FROM MIDDLESEX VOL I

Edited by Simon Harwin

First published in Great Britain in 2000 by
YOUNG WRITERS
Remus House,
Coltsfoot Drive,
Woodston,
Peterborough, PE2 9JX
Telephone (01733) 890066

HB ISBN 0 75431 932 6
SB ISBN 0 75431 933 4

FOREWORD

This year, the Young Writers' Future Voices competition proudly presents a showcase of the best poetic talent from over 42,000 up-and-coming writers nationwide.

Successful in continuing our aim of promoting writing and creativity in children, our regional anthologies give a vivid insight into the thoughts, emotions and experiences of today's younger generation, displaying their inventive writing in its originality.

The thought, effort, imagination and hard work put into each poem impressed us all and again the task of editing proved challenging due to the quality of entries received, but was nevertheless enjoyable. We hope you are as pleased as we are with the final selection and that you continue to enjoy *Future Voices From Middlesex Vol I* for many years to come.

CONTENTS

Enfield County School

Romona Miller	19
Aisha Sommerville	19
Catherine Ardill	20
Yioda Andreou	21
Natalie Maraj	21
Sebrina Murray	22
Stacey Goldsworthy	23
Emma Howard	24
Donna Skerratt	24
Kate Lyne	25
Kathryn Taylor	26
Gemma Brock	26
Joanne Holmes	27
Natasha Constandinou	28
Halina Watts	28
Nazan Fikret	29
Shema Najib	30
Roshni Patel	30
Melissa Brown	31
Zena Evangelou	32
Zoe Reinhart	33
Charlotte Bill	33
Alanna Blaney	34

Feltham Community College

Stacey Leanne Maycock	34
Nadine Hanson	35
Laura Scarrott	35
Carlie Rodney	36
Rebecca Garnett	37
Leigh Kettles	38
Marc Ellix	38
Russell Clow	39
Danielle Welland	40
Aaron King	40
Sascha Finn	41
David Enstone	42

Longford Community School

Roxanne Winton	66
Jodie Wells	66
Jason Bona	67
Kylie Sutton	67
Kelly Anderson	68
Mary Reilly	68
Aaron Fullick	69
Elizabeth Franklyn	69
Shannon Deal	69
Sara Wood	70
Komal Anwar	70
Vicky Bhyat	71

Northwood School

Joanna Hossack	71
Thomas Melton	72
Jennifer Yarrow	72
Philip J Grehan	73
Daniel O'Brien	73
Alice Walsh	74
Greg Townsin	74
Alex Baulch	75
Adrienne Heath	75
Angharad Birtles	76
Amy Sawtell	77
Dan Fortella	77
Jodie Simmons	78
Kayleigh Thomas	78
Kelly Whoriskey	79
Kimberley Robson	80
Philippa Monypenny	80
Toni Emma Metcalf	81
Devan Pankhania	81
Ushma Mistry	82
Abdul Malik	82
Mohammed Basma	83
Kate Balkin	84
Luke Colwill	84

Nicholas Borton	85
Jamie-Lee Lover	85
Lee Collum	86
Holly Frost	86

Preston Manor High School

Manish Kerai	87
Himesh Tailor	87
Tala Holmes-Gouveia	88
Jharna Bhatia	88
Peter Lewinson	89
Junaid Manzoor	89
Simone Austin	90
Heemali Patel	91
Mili Patel	91
Shima Parbat	92
Nimisha Thakor	92
Hershika Kerai	93
Eugene Anderson	93
Princess Omonira	94
Caprisha Pennant	95
Geeta Patel	96
Bhirel Patel	97
Shiraz Akhtar	97
Bijal Tailor	98
Heena Pindoria	98
Michael Etsey Jnr	99
Moeen Khan	99
Sofia Sheikh	100
Ashok Varsani	100
Dipika Vagjiani	101
Cherrelle Francis	101
Kanika Royer	102
Anil Patel	102
Ann Marie Morrison	103
Mansha Varsani	104
Reena Patel	104
Manesh Mistry	105

The Poems

MY FEELINGS

No day is colourful
Without you
It seems all dark.

Time would go by
But your love will stay with me
In my heart deep down
I will always love you.

However long it takes
I will still love you forever
Until you come back to me.

Please God don't leave
My love to waste.

Sundeep Kaur Gill

FRIENDS

Friends are people, who can be there for you,
You can't take them for granted
And they can't do that to you.

You should be there for each other,
Helping hand in hand,
Never break the promises,
Which you made on this land.

If you've got a friend,
You have a treasure,
But please remember,
To be there forever.

Puneeta Sharma (13)

LOVE HURTS

Just watching you on a sunny day
walking past . . . beautiful
just watching you on a sunny day
walking past . . . painful.

You are my sunshine after the rain
you are the care against my
fear and pain.

'Cos I'm losing my mind when
You're not around.
It's all because of you.

Honestly could it be you and me
like it was now
neither less or more.

'Cos when I close my eyes at night
I realise that no one else could
ever take your place.

It's just in the sun where our love began . . .

Bushra Khan (14)

LOVE!

Love is not in this real world,
Love is in another place,
In a fantasy in some other world,
A world where I meet you,
Where I hold you in my arms.
Where I have you in front of my eyes
And in this love I want to stay this way
Just you and me and another day gone by!

Hina Ali (12)

SIMONE THE SNAKE

Shh! Shh! Shh!
Simone the snake,
Oh! The fuss he makes
To catch his prey
And to obey.

Shh! Shh! Shh!
Simone the snake,
Oh! How long will he take
As he creeps
And then he leaps
So he can have his feast.

Shh! Shh! Shh!
Simone the snake,
At last he has made it
He thinks it's a piece of cake
As he has his nap
And then he wears a cap.

Priyanka Chandorkar (11)
Alperton Community School

A POEM ABOUT TIGERS

Tiger, tiger, you're fierce,
Tiger, you are orange and black,
Tiger, you live in the jungle,
Tiger, you are a meat eater,
Tiger, you are a four-legged animal,
Tigers are killers and fast animals.

Bhavesh Varsani (11)
Alperton Community School

POP THE PANDA

Crunch! Crunch! Crunch!
Pop the panda left her tree,
Looking for bamboo
Look left, look right, look all around,
Is anyone there?
Rustle! Rustle! Rustle!
What was that?
Who's that behind the bushes?
Look left, look right, look all around,
What shall I do?
Bang! Bang! Bang!
Where will I go?
Oh deary me, he's shooting at me!
Look left, look right, look all around,
Better get a move on.
Run! Run! Run!
Won't this guy give up?
Jump in the bushes quickly!
Look left, look right, look all around.
Gosh he's close!
Better get a move on.

Leila Kimberly Chauhan (11)
Alperton Community School

WHISTLING AND CLICKING, WHISTLE AND CLICK

Whistling and clicking, whistle and click,
Dolphins jump over, so high, so quick,
Under the water, over the water,
Whistling and clicking, whistle and click.

Whistling and clicking, whistle and click,
Swimming as the waves go by,
Close by to people as they laugh and sigh,
Whistling and clicking, whistle and click.

Gliding through the deep, deep water,
Eating fish to fill your tum,
Down, down, down, down it goes
Gliding through the deep, deep water.

Whistling and clicking, whistle and click,
Dolphins jump over, so high, so quick,
Under the water, over the water,
Whistling and clicking, whistle and click.

Umisha Hirani (11)
Alperton Community School

DINO THE DINOSAUR

Its skin is rough, rough as sandpaper,
It is heavy, terrific and scary.
It likes it when it sees its prey,
Cos it gulps its food down, in one go!
So beware!
It could be there.

The dinosaur shakes the whole world,
Because of its huge strides.
It is as tall as a two hundred storey building
And it can gulp its food down in one go.
So beware!
It could be there.

It is not very friendly, nor very kind.
The earth to the dinosaur,
Is just like a ball,
Which it can eat!
So beware!
It could be there.

Ritesh Dass (11)
Alperton Community School

THE RABBIT

Rabbit, oh rabbit, with a tail that's so bushy
With big, wide eyes,
With a nose that's so swishy.

Rabbit, oh rabbit, your face is so spotty,
He always hops around and leaves things so messy.

She's white as snow, so I call her Snowy
But sometimes she feels different,
So she likes to be called Chloe.

She loves to be stroked and held all the time
But when she smells food
She knows it's supper time.

Kyeesiha Teri Jacobs (11)
Alperton Community School

BILLY BAT

Billy bat,
As silent as grass
Motionless when sleeping
Tears when weeping.

Billy bat is sweet and cool,
He tries so hard
But he can't seem to stop his drool
This bat likes to eat loud.

Billy bat is black as coal
He can see at night
But can't see when he's in a fright
He is just as blind as a bat he is.

Nund Vyas (11)
Alperton Community School

SILENT SWAN

Silent swan! Silent swan!
Gliding along the water in the most graceful fashion,
Looking at the other swans as they glide by,
But where are you going?
Where are you going?

Silent swan! Silent swan!
A swan with a red brown beak
A swan with webbed feet
But where are you going?
Where are you going?

Silent swan! Silent swan!
She's going to see her baby swans
Grey baby swans
So that's where you are going?

Sheena Bhuva (11)
Alperton Community School

RATTLESNAKE

Rattle, rattle, rattle
There the snake goes over the hills,
To find its prey.
Rattle, rattle, rattle
There it goes
Wonder how fast it can go?
Rattle, rattle, rattle,
Down it goes
Down it goes
To rest its bones.

Matthew Amoo (11)
Alperton Community School

RHINO

Rhino is the name of my reptile,
Rhino, Rhino, the fat rhino.
White, green skin and a black eye
Like a dinosaur's.
Rhino has four legs
Rhino, Rhino,
Rhino, the slowest rhino
And the rhino which is the hungriest.
This rhino, rhino,
Lives in a beautiful land.
Rhino is slow and fat,
That's why people thrive,
That rhino is the worst.
Rhino is feeling very cold
As I told you
He lives in a land
Rhino, Rhino, the bad rhino.

Sneha Desai (11)
Alperton Community School

MOUSE

There is no place to hide!
You must run for your life,
Or be cut into pieces and eaten!
Run as fast as your legs take you!
Get into that tiny hole.

I am tiny and not strong,
I have sharp teeth
I have no mother or father,
I am dying of starvation,
There is no cheese to eat!

She is a nasty brat,
Who is always chasing me
She has nothing better to do
Look at her eating cat food!
But there is no cheese for me.

Kalpa Shah (12)
Alperton Community School

RACHEL THE RABBIT

Munch! Munch! Munch!
Came Rachel the rabbit,
From her burrow
Guess what she saw?

She saw a fox,
She didn't know
What to do
Then she scratched her nails on the wall.

The squeaky noise scared the
Fox, she scared the fox off.
She laughed
And laughed.

When she opened her eyes
She saw the fox
Has run far away
Away in the distance.

The next day
When Rachel came out
To do her shopping
She saw the fox!

Hina Patel (12)
Alperton Community School

MOUSE'S NEST

I found a ball of grass among the hay
And prodded it as I passed and went away
And when I looked again something stirred.
I turned again and hopped to catch the bird
When out an old mouse bolted in the wheat,
With all her young ones hanging at her toes.
She looked so cold and so grotesque to me,
I ran and wondered what the thing could be
And pushed the ??? bunches where I stood.
Then the mouse hurried from the cracking broad
The young ones squeaked and as I went away
She found her nest again among the hay.
Then water o'er the pebbles began to run
And broad old ??? pools glittered in the sun.

Nitin Suriacant (11)
Alperton Community School

MY DOG DIED

My dog died last winter,
He died of chill and cold,
I don't know what to do now,
I feel so alone.
He played with me every day
We had lots of fun together,
He was my best friend
And I was his,
But now he's gone
What shall I do?

Kaushal Pindoria (11)
Alperton Community School

ERIC THE ELEPHANT

Eric the elephant is huge and tall,
He always likes to lean on the wall.
His legs are thick, very, very thick.
He stands in the water and tries to kick.

Eric the elephant looks for food and tries to leap,
But, when you see him, he's fast asleep.
He likes to eat fresh meat
But, he's always eating wet wheat.

Eric the elephant walks with big strides,
He's always giving people rides.
Everyone likes him very, very much,
He's a big animal with a lovingly touch.

Pritesh Kalyan (11)
Alperton Community School

FRED THE FROG

There was a frog called Fred
He was coloured dark red,
Fred has a friend called Ben
Who was ten.

They loved to play with a ball
On top of a red wall,
One day they fell
Into a deep well.

Then Fred and Ben got out
They took back their ball,
They said, 'I am never playing again.'
Then they went home.

Hiren Gami (11)
Alperton Community School

Visitor From Space

The alien came down to Earth.
I came out the house.
The alien came out of his ship
And said 'Hello.'
He came into the house and ate some pizza
He then flew home
Where did he go?
Was it Mars?
Or was it Jupiter?
We will never know
We will never know.

Ben Parrish (11)
Chantry School

Fur Coats

F   ur should stay on animals
U   nder their fur, they are like human beings
R   unning in the wild, free like we do.

C   ost is not the matter, animals are the matter
O   nly if humans would stop and think
A   ouch! Aouch! The animals are crying
T   hink how much nicer animals look with their fur
S   top the animal cruelty.

Sundeep Gill (12)
Chantry School

AN ALIEN'S LIFE

An alien leads a very strange life.
Never will he understand another language
Actually he don't have a wife.

Life for an alien is very short
In fact many life years for an alien is thirty
Extraordinary!

Now the alien is thirty-nine

Strange things could happen
Near the deadline!
Looking forward is very sad.

In one year's time, things will be very bad
Friendly people reaching out
Encourages a friendship there is no doubt.

Suddenly, it's time to go and the mournful bell
Chimes very slowly.

All the people have to shout
They just can't stand it
They had to pout.

Mark Knight (11)
Chantry School

WHY DO THEY DO IT?

Animals are gentle creatures
Living in the wild
People treat them really bad
Why do they do it?

Animals are gentle creatures
Caged in the zoo
No escape, people looking
Why do they do it?

Animals are gentle creatures
Living in the jungle
People with guns hunting
Why do they do it?

Animals are gentle creatures
Fish swimming in rivers and lakes
No peace, hooks stuck in them
Why do they do it?

Animals are gentle creatures
People should care
No more hurting them
Why do they do it?

Colin Mills (12)
Chantry School

ANIMALS

Animals are here
Animals are there
Animals are everywhere
When the alien came down to stay
All the animals ran away
Aliens are green
Bats are black
That's the world it works like that
When I say my mum, that day
She said, 'Some visitors are going to stay.'
I asked who they were,
She said, 'They're green'
I asked again
She said, 'They're mean.'
I said 'Mum who are they?'
She said, 'They're bad!'
I asked again she said, 'They're mad!'
The green aliens are here to stay
And so we all must play, play, play . . .
Ah ah . . .

Daryl Tyler (11)
Chantry School

ANIMALS

A   nimals are nice and fluffy
N   ot all are scruffy
I   'm not an animal fan
M   any people are fans
A   nyone for a rabbit
L   ovely and tender
S   o soft and small will easily surrender.

Lloyd Dundas (12)
Chantry School

A Hallowe'en Poem

Happy and fun time for everyone
Around about nine at night you should get a fright
Laughter and fun for everyone
Laughs are heard all around
And when it's late, not a sound.
Out and about the children scout.
Witches, goblins and ghosts for
That night, are our special hosts.
End of the day is the best so stay
Ending is near, so do not fear
I will see you again same time next year
Not to scream, it's never a dream
When it comes to Hallowe'en.

Jamie Sheriff (12)
Chantry School

Animals

A nimals can be vicious or they can be cute,
N early all the land where animals live is gone,
I ce is melting earthquakes and storms,
M an is destroying animals and themselves like the dinosaurs
A nd conga's are dying,
L ots of tigers dead, poachers killing them
S ome nature reserves are breeding animals to increase numbers
so that the food chain is back in order.

Rory McKenzie (12)
Chantry School

GREYHOUND RACING

Once upon a time there was a greyhound
Her name was Monroe Slippy
She was a fast dog. She won lots of races
She was born and bred in Ireland.
At sixteen months she came to England
At twenty months my dad bought her
She came first in the heats
First in the final
It was a great night.

Ryan Malin (12)
Chantry School

HALLOWE'EN

Hallowe'en, Hallowe'en, it is dark,
Little children door to door
Getting lots of candy
Lots of witches and goblins too.

Hallowe'en, Hallowe'en, it is the end
It is a good one, wait till the next one
Hallowe'en, Hallowe'en
It is here again.

Tony McCarthy (13)
Chantry School

HALLOWE'EN

Ghouls and goblins, witches and cats
But beware of vampire bats
Hallowe'en night is here
Full of terror, full of fear.

Don't go out when the skies are black
You don't ever know what's going to attack
Don't walk the streets, don't go to the door
As the ghouls and goblins will get you for sure.

Don't try to make a witches brew
Or else they will come after you
Don't tamper with the other side
Unless you have some place to hide.

Hallowe'en is a night for the dead to come back
So be careful what you put in your trick or treat sack
You could get a hand; you could get a nail
You could even get something with a terrible smell.

So be cautious be aware
If you are one to easily scare
The trick and treats might be not what you expect
You never know what's going to come next.

Wesley Shillingford (13)
Chantry School

LUCKY TO BE ALIVE

Black, white, Indian or from Japan,
We all have friends, make the most if you can
Tall, short, skinny or fat
Do we all care oh no not that.
Youth, confidence, breath and life
My got up has gone to meet my wife.
Ugly, old, wrinkled all up
I lie in bed cos I cannot get up
With my ears in a drawer
And my teeth in a cup
My specs on the table until I get up,
Eyes gone grey, skin gone pale
Sometimes I wonder if I'm going stale.
Injections and tablets to help me stay alive
But I am lucky to be alive.

Romona Miller (12)
Enfield County School

THE OLD MAN

Everywhere I go,
Everyone I see,
People always judge me for what I appear to be
I know I may be ugly with big black bags
I know I am dressed in dirty rags.

My tuffs of hair are all grey
I feel older every day
My dentures smell like rotten fish
I wish I could be a beautiful prince.

Aisha Sommerville (12)
Enfield County School

UNWELCOME

I went by the church and heard bells ringing,
Followed by the sound of someone singing.
I followed the noise and found them there
All I could do was stand and stare.
Frankenstein's monster was singing a song
Accompanied by Mr Hyde, Dracula and a zombie called Gong.
I backed away, very scared, by then they called me over,
Gong nearly knocked me out with his cello, the size of Dover.
They looked so sad, so I asked them why.
Mr Hyde fell at my feet and began to cry.
'Everybody's scared of us,' the monster said.
'It makes us so depressed we just want to crawl under our beds,
Look at Dracula standing over there,
He's so kind and caring but people just stop and stare
And Frankenstein's monster so warm and lovely.
But people just think he's weird and ugly
And poor old Gong he's not so bad.
But people run away from him, it makes him so sad
And then there's me, I'm warm at heart
But I've always been given the Psycho part.'
And so I walked away feeling so sad,
I think why people can treat them so bad.
And so I thought as I stood in the cold
I'd go out and show the world.
That people like them have been created
Into something so bad that they're all hated.
So the next day I told everyone, that
All they want is a place under the sun.
So now everyone sees them a different way
They won't be driven out, they'll feel welcome and stay.

Catherine Ardill (12)
Enfield County School

BE MY FRIEND

I'm not as I appear to be
I'm kind and soft
Not as you see
I'd like you to understand me
And be the friend I want you to be.

One day I would like to jump with glee
Because somebody played with me
Let me out, let me be free
Let me be the person, I want to be.
I wish that somebody would love me
I don't like it when I'm unhappy
I'd like you to understand me
And be the friend I want you to be.

Yioda Andreou (12)
Enfield County School

THE MONSTER UNDER MY BED

Every night I hear a noise under my bed,
'There's nothing there' my mum said,
I closed my eyes and fell asleep,
Then woke up again and thought I'll take a peep,
I held my breath and pulled up the covers,
Something big, something hairy, suddenly
Jumped out the cupboard,
The big hairy monster jumped on my bed and licked me.
I turned on my lamp and it was Jessy my black cat
I stroked her thin black coat as she
Let out a long soft purr.

Natalie Maraj (12)
Enfield County School

LONELY CHILD

There is a girl at my school,
Who's always upset
But I don't have a clue.

She's always alone and quiet,
So I wonder if she'll ever get through.

I saw her alone walking down the streets,
I ran up to her
And she cried on me.

I said to her,
'Are you alright?'
She announced back
'Would you come with me,'

I went to her house
It was big and clean
She went upstairs so I went too.

I followed her to a dark little room
It was so small like a little shoe.

She saw I was there and pushed me out
And shouted out 'Get out, get out!'

I got down the stairs and she came too,
With an album of pictures
Of people she said she never knew.

When we had something to eat she then told me,
I was adopted
To these parents who are mean.

I said to her,
'You poor little thing,'
And now I know
Why she's always sad and lonely.

Sebrina Murray (12)
Enfield County School

RAINBOW

I saw my first rainbow when I was one,
My mum told me to run,
So I ran and I ran, I thought to myself why am I running?
But my mum shouted out 'Keep on running.'

I saw my second rainbow when I was three,
I was with my brother up in a tree.
He told me to fly up into the sky
I thought to myself, I wonder why?
But my brother shouted out,
'Go and fly up into the sky.'

I saw my fourth rainbow when I was seven
I asked my mum, 'Do I have to run?'
She said 'No but go catch that sun,'
No way, I will get wet from the rain.

I saw my seventh rainbow when I was twelve,
I asked my brother if I had to fly
He said, 'No way,' so I said
'Why did I have to fly when I was three.'
He said 'Because we're up in a tree.'

Stacey Goldsworthy (12)
Enfield County School

WHAT LIFE WAS MEANT TO BE!

I'm only someone with feelings like you
I might be ugly on the outside,
But I'm pretty on the inside.
I'm kind, generous but no one cares,
They think I'm horrible, mean and spiteful,
But I'm not, I'm just like you
People look at me and run away
And all I want to do is play.
Let me be human,
Then you will see the true me.
I've always wanted to see
What life was meant to be!

Emma Howard (12)
Enfield County School

BEST FRIENDS

My best friend is Kate
She's the bestest mate.
When we go out she's never late,
She's a great mate.
She laughs at my jokes
She calls on the phone
When it opens we're going to the Dome.
When I hear Kate, it brings a smile to my face,
She's the bestest mate,
I hope we never break, it would be fate.

Donna Skerratt (12)
Enfield County School

SEASONS

The autumn mist is coming
Covering up the deep blue sky
The warm sunshine is going
And the birds are about to fly.
The leaves are slowly falling
Golden, crisp and brown
The conker season's over
It's like a merry-go-round.

The woolly hats and gloves are out,
Preparing for a chill
Winter is here
Ready to kill
Everybody's waiting
For the crisp white snow
To get outside and collect it up
Ready for a show.

New life is beginning
Things are being born
Lambs are slowly rising
With lots of things before them.
Young children are smiling
Knowing what's in store
Easter eggs are popular
Chocolate is galore.

The holiday season's with us all
Everybody's glad
The paddling pool's being filled
Filled with lots of fun
Everybody's splashing around
In the hot sun.

Kate Lyne (12)
Enfield County School

WEATHER

Wait for the rain to come out,
Play in the rain
And it will rain all day
The sky is grey
Has the sun come out? No.
Play in the rain
Rain, rain, rain.

Rain, rain, rain,
Play outside in the rain,
There are puddles everywhere
The trees stand in waves everywhere
Rain, rain is everywhere.

Rain, rain is everywhere,
I like it when the rain is loud
When I am inside,
I like to see lots of rain,
Go into a puddle.
I love it when I splash
In puddles.

Kathryn Taylor (12)
Enfield County School

THE LONELY MONSTER

Why do these people judge me by my looks?
They don't look inside me,
If only they would.

Why do these people stop and stare?
If only they knew,
How much I care.

Why do these people treat me so badly?
If only they'd change,
I'd accept it gladly.

Why do these people do this to me?
If only they knew,
What it's like to be me.

Gemma Brock (13)
Enfield County School

BRIGHT RED SOCKS

Last year at home, I was very sad,
And my grades at school were really bad!
Then for Christmas, in a big, fat box,
I got a pair of bright red socks!

'Hooray! Hooray! I yelled out loud,
'Cause with my socks, I was really proud!
I wore them to school every day,
And my grades improved to a perfect 'A'!

Then in PE, which was five minutes long,
I discovered that those socks had gone!
I held my breath and walked away,
Wondering what my mum would say!

I got home that night, feeling like a mug,
My mum greeted me with a great big hug!
I told her about my missing socks,
And she presented me with another big box!

I opened it, the light blue box,
It was another pair of bright red socks!

Joanne Holmes (12)
Enfield County School

SHADOW MEN

I closed my eyes and fell,
Slipped again on those slime-stained stones,
To that murky place by rusty fire lit,
Where they lie fingering old bones.
Go with my fear, deep into the pit,
Dreadful truths I'm told, though always with cost.
I play their games like the other fools who've slipped on
                          those same stones,
And played and lost.
I come because I must,
I have no choice.
Anger and fear are their mad lust,
And the power of darkness is their voice.
They chase me with pleasured hate all through the night,
Until light of day threatens their black fright.
At last I leave them, waiting there below,
I can hear them laughing as I go.

Natasha Constandinou (12)
Enfield County School

FRANKENSTEIN

I have a name,
But no one knows it.
I have a face,
But no one sees it.
Me the person who
Is known as bad,
Feels scared and lonely
And very sad!

Halina Watts (12)
Enfield County School

LONELINESS

If you think you are lonely
Then listen closely do,
I will now tell you a tale of an old man that I once knew . . .

He was born and bred in Liverpool
Where his life was so mean and cruel,
At ten he was sent to a workhouse
With no one to miss him at all.

He slaved for a Mr Flincher,
He worked all day and night
He dwelled in the mill house
Living in such plight.

At fourteen he left the workhouse
With memories depressing,
He had many cuts and bruises
Without any dressing.

He walked for months on end,
For I shall not pretend,
His life was one of many
Of people without any.

For years he lived on streets,
Not making ends meet,
He begged for food all day
For warmth and somewhere to stay.

And that is how I met him,
The old men I once knew,
For if I saw you lonely
I would be sure to help you too . . .

Nazan Fikret (12)
Enfield County School

MONSTER

I'm a monster
Sad and lonely,
I'm ugly, yellow, tall and bony
My face is covered in matted black hair,
My eyes are hideous and red rimmed with care
I'm a hunchback who wears simple breeches
I'm naked to the waste and have a good taste,
I have a waxy face and black lips and
Scars cross my cheeks.

I'm not bad, I'm really kind
Just because I'm different you all mind,
If you look deep down,
You'll see that I'm safe and sound,
Nobody likes me, can't you see
It's only because I'm ugly.

Shema Najib (12)
Enfield County School

THE OUTSIDE WORLD

I lie alone on my bed,
Wondering what's going on
In the outside world
Where I haven't been for God knows how long!

Is the day ending or has it just begun?
I wonder, is anyone missing me or have they just forgotten?

I guess it doesn't matter
What's going on,
As I'm not going out there soon.
I haven't been for so long.

Roshni Patel (12)
Enfield County School

THE PERFORMANCE

Excitement grows behind the stage,
The audience holds people of every age.
'Testing, testing, 1, 2, 3,'
I hope that everyone can see.
This needs to be good for young and old,
Our routine yet again begins to unfold.
Then, while our stomachs have butterflies,
To our coach the last goodbyes . . .
Then we're out! Dancers are everywhere,
Costumes and make-up, and beautiful hair,
They're flying everywhere
Without a care.
The show's getting going now,
Though I did question how.
Whilst I'm dancing around crazily,
I silently reminisce hazily
Over good times and bad,
Over happy and sad.
Time whizzes by, though I'm having fun,
It seems like the show's only just begun.
But soon we're running fast to backstage,
Compared to out there, it seems like a cage.
I laugh and rejoice with all of my friends,
At least our friendship never ends.

Melissa Brown (12)
Enfield County School

LIFE

What is life?
Is it big or is it small?
Is it long or is it short?
What is life?

Life is fun,
Life is sad,
Life is bad,
Life is sad.

What is life?
You have to take chances in life,
You have to really be ready for a fight.
What is life?

Life is worth everything,
Just sit down and have a think,
Friends,
Parents,
Brothers,
Sisters,
You need them all in whatever the circumstances.

I'll never know what the meaning of life is,
But I have every reason to live.

Zena Evangelou (12)
Enfield County School

MONSTER POEM

I came into the world knowing nothing.
All I wanted was to live in peace and harmony with everyone.
I never thought that people could be so cruel.
I try to make friends but all that people are bothered
      about is themselves and how people look.
Surely, how you look on the outside doesn't matter?
I am a very caring person inside.
No one has helped me, this world seems to be a terrible place.
No one has cared for me, this is a disgrace to the human race.
No one loves me, I only want to have some fun.
No one loves me, what have I done?
Will you be my friend?

Zoe Reinhart (12)
Enfield County School

MY NEXT DOOR NEIGHBOUR

My next door neighbour is really weird,
And by most people is very much feared.
She has long black hair and big brown eyes,
If you bump into her, you'll have a surprise.
She's tall, she's scary and very hairy,
But nobody knows her like me.
She's kind and loving and very nice,
She cooks you dinner, your favourite chilli con carne and rice.
If you get to know her you'll understand what I mean,
She's nice inside and very keen.

Charlotte Bill (13)
Enfield County School

Society's Creation

I am society's creation,
I am society's mind,
Distorted and assorted,
In this innocent child.

My mind is a blank sheet
Which you fill with your art.
Too young to appreciate the corruption
I suffer in mind and heart.

Is your easel filled with hate,
The suffering of years?
Your sick twisted pleasures,
Of others' paranoid fears?

I am society's creation
If not careful, society's ills,
I am your creation.
Have you taught me how to kill?

Alanna Blaney (13)
Enfield County School

Winter

Trees are all bare
With their coats taken
Something in the air
That's about to waken.

The colours of the clouds
White, grey and yellow
As I walk towards home
Everything seems mellow.

Stacey Leanne Maycock (11)
Feltham Community College

IT WAS

It was so silent I could hear
the blink of an ant's eye,
the beat of a heart.

It was so peaceful that I heard
the leaves as they fell
to the ground.

It was so still that I could hear
the yawn of the sinking sun and
the rising moon.

It was so silent I could hear the
floor scream each time someone
took a step.

It was so silent I could hear
the sun speaking to the clouds saying
'Don't rain yet, my time isn't up . . .'

Nadine Hanson (12)
Feltham Community College

IT WAS . . .

It was so silent that I heard the
gentle yawn of a sinking sun.

It was so peaceful that I heard
a singing leaf swaying in the breeze.

It was so still that I sensed a sun's
beam dancing in the light.

It was so silent that I heard the
never-ending moan of a closing book.

Laura Scarrott (12)
Feltham Community College

MY SEASIDE SONG

It was a blue sky
Birds were flying high
Streaming sun
Ready for lots of fun
Kind of day.

There was a big slide, a swimming pool
All the big kids acting cool.
Kids scream for ice cream
While their fathers sit and dream.

We had a great week, not much sleep
Aching feet
From walking through the pebbles.

Seashells glimmer in the light
While my brothers squabble and fight
The sea was blue and very gay
I watched the children wildly play.

The rides were fun, the bubblegum,
The flavours that they had;
Cherry rum, orange gum,
Strawberry banana bluster,
Chocolate chip suey cluster
Coca mocha macaroni
Tapioca smoked baloney
All these flavours you could pick
But oh my, did it make you sick!

It was the best time, the greatest time
A triple slickle pickle time
The places to go, the places we went
We even had a crazy golf course to rent.

We never got bored there was always
                    something to do
We had a food dish, swam with fish
Big ones, small ones, big gigantic colourful ones
The sights we saw on the shore
Made you think you were in heaven
But here we are on the plane
                    on our way back home to Devon!

Carlie Rodney (12)
Feltham Community College

My Seaside Song

It was a fun-filled, ferris wheel,
Soft sand, sticky hand,
Loads of arcades, sandwich full of marmalade,
Kind of town.

We ate fish and chips,
Stuffed food through our lips,
And ate ice-creams all through the day.

We swam in the sea, till it was time for tea.
We played cricket all day, on the sandy bay,
And Mum laid on the sand, waiting for her tan.

We saw seagulls, people playing bowls,
Children having fun, screaming in the sun
The smell of fresh fish, on a chipful dish.

At the end of the day, we said bye to the bay.
We went back home, near the Millennium Dome.
We counted the sheep, then fell asleep,
On the way home to London.

Rebecca Garnett (12)
Feltham Community College

MY DAY OUT

Aquatic water park in France,
St Tropez was where I was
on a cold stormy day.
There was fork lightning,
it was very frightening.
I was stuck in an arcade
wearing only a bikini.
My feet were freezing,
little kids screaming.
I couldn't speak French to
ask of the time.
I was about to whine till
I saw the sunshine
It was great because there
were no queues on rides.
My best was where
you sit side by side.
It is called 'Rapids Rouge'
which means 'Rapids Red'
I couldn't wait to get home
and eat a nice box of chips.

Leigh Kettles (12)
Feltham Community College

SUMMER HOLIDAYS

Holiday, holiday
Time to play.
Fun in the park
Ice-creams all day.
Six weeks of fun.
No school for ages.
You just look up 'Fun'
in the Yellow Pages.

Holiday, holiday
Jetting away
To the Middle East
Or the USA.
You may find it cold
You may find it hot
Just get a six-pack of beer
And a nice shady spot!

Marc Ellix (12)
Feltham Community College

IT WAS

It was so silent, I could hear
The whispering of
The clouds.

It was so peaceful, I could hear
A bird's feather
Flap in the wind.

It was so quiet, I could hear
An ant's march
Of silent steps.

It was so quiet, I could hear
The movements of the clouds
In the air.

It was so silent, I could hear
The flapping of
A fly's wing.

It was so silent, I could hear
Myself
Think!

Russell Clow (12)
Feltham Community College

SUMMER HOLIDAY POEM

Summer has come
Children have fun
Playing around in the sun
Thinking of all that they've done.

I went to Jersey
But didn't visit Guernsey
Went to Pearl's
And got no curls.

Went to the zoo
But didn't see Sue.
Went to the underground hospital
But saw no Germans at all.

Went to Treasures of the Earth
But didn't visit Perth.
Went to the beach
But didn't eat a peach.

Went to the shell garden
And didn't say pardon.
Went to the lifeboat
And didn't wear a coat.

Danielle Welland (12)
Feltham Community College

QUIETLY DOES IT . . .

It was so silent I could hear the movement of a cloud,
with the burning of the sun.

It was so still that I heard the steady blowing of air
and the wings of a ladybird flying in the sky.

It was so peaceful I could hear the fish blowing bubbles
as the sea echoed with beautiful sounds.

It was so silent I could hear the slug's sticky trail
being left behind as it left the green grass.

Aaron King (12)
Feltham Community College

MY DAY OUT

We all jumped in the car, excited!
Because we were going to Alton Towers.
We were half way there, still excited,
But there was a case of heavy showers!
We were nearly there, bored!
And goodness what a queue!
We were finally there, really bored!
'Mum, I need the loo!'
We queued up for hours, really bored,
Eating chocolate and cheesy crisps!
We finally got in, thank God!
But most rides were closed, what had we missed?
We waited under a shelter, angry,
And bought a lolly to suck,
We were getting sick, (yawn)
Of the smell of vinegar, yuk!
We went back to the car, angry,
Half way there we broke down.
We waited for Grandad, patiently,
And he turned up with a frown.
He fixed the car, thankfully,
And we finished our journey home,
And when we got there, (home that is!)
Out came the sun! (Groan.)

Sascha Finn (12)
Feltham Community College

IT WAS SO SILENT

It was so silent I could hear
The snoring of a turned off lamp
Like a pig grunting for food . . .

It was so peaceful I could hear
The singing of pansies as the bright light
                              shone upon them
A merry joyful song

It was so still I could hear
The crying of pain from the floor as a step was taken
Teardrops running down the floor evaporating quickly.

It was so quiet I could hear
A hippo wanting some cake
Screaming as loudly as he could.

It was so peaceful I could hear
Steven's mind telling him not to play football
Trying to disagree with it.

It was so still I could hear
The sun screaming for a fire extinguisher
But everyone letting him burn

It was so quiet I could hear
The nattering of squirrels' teeth
Gnashing a dark brown nut.

It was so silent!

David Enstone (12)
Feltham Community College

IT WAS SO SILENT, I COULD HEAR

It was so silent I could hear
A bird puff and pant,
The slither of a snake
The ground I trod, quake.

A pin hit the floor,
The squeak of a door
A bird flying high
The closing of an eye.

A lonely fish swim
The lights growing dim
The snow hit the ground
Every single sound.

Nicholas Crawford (12)
Feltham Community College

ANGER

The final whistle has gone,
We have lost again,
This time it's against Chelsea
It's driving me round the bend.

We've had two managers already
Ruud Gullit and Bobby Robson,
The second still has to prove himself,
I hope he does it soon.

Sheffield Wednesday are below us,
I hope it stays that way,
We should win against them,
I hope we do anyway.

Steven Stewart (12)
Feltham Community College

MILLENNIUM THE WRONG WAY

Imagine the millennium the wrong way,
lights flicking, flashing, slowly dying out,
blackouts, sky moving, earth moving,
eating and chewing the world piece by piece.
Ice age, heaters up and gas bill rising,
do you think the millennium like that?
In a way that's what I think,
predictions and theories,
so many of them, one's bound to be right,
but we may put these down to nothing.
We can never be sure what is going to happen until we're there.
You may be already there reading this in the millennium
and you maybe thinking I was making it all up,
but we just never know what the future holds.

Toby Davies (11)
Feltham Community College

SUMMER HOLIDAY POEM

This summer holiday was pretty flash
I've started a paper round so I'm earning more cash
After I've finished my hands are black
They're as black as a witch's black cat.

Also this holiday I went to Thorpe Park
We stayed late, we went when it was dark.
When we went I was tired, but sad all the same
I'm definitely sure I'm glad I came.

I think the holiday did go fast,
Much much faster than the past.
But overall it was OK,
I'm looking forward to next year's summer holiday.

Mark Wilby (13)
Feltham Community College

IT WAS

It was so silent
I could hear the thumping of ants marching
Like my heart beating after a long run.

It was so peaceful
I could hear the waves whistling
And the crackle of the cliffs being eroded away.

It was so still
I was able to hear
The plants stretching towards the sun.

It was so quiet
That I could hear a mouse snoring
Through a nightmare about cats.

It was so silent
I heard someone's hairs growing
In an attempt to grow longer than the other hairs.

It was so peaceful
I could hear brain cells
Tackling a hard sum.

It was so still
That I could hear my bones
Resting as I slept in my bed.

Emily Flanagan (12)
Feltham Community College

IT WAS SO . . .

It was so silent that I heard
army ants
preparing for war.

It was so silent that I heard
the sun talking
to the clouds.

It was so peaceful I heard
the clock groaning
'My arms ache.'

It was so still I sensed
dust gliding in the wind.

It was so silent I heard
a blade of grass
sighing in the wind.

Harry Malins (12)
Feltham Community College

MY SEASIDE WHACKER OF A POEM

It was a
water bursting, scuba diving, wind surfing,
water skiing, speed boating, wave splashing, sunny
summer's day.

It was a
sand swirling, castle building, sun scorching, crab catching,
children swarming, ball bouncing, hole digging, deck chairs collapsing,
people burning, sun cream melting, down at the beach in Whittering.

It was a
chip chewing, sweat sucking, rock chomping, coke sipping,
belly bloating, ice melting, band stand standing, cash spending,
Punch and Judy showing, shouting, screaming, shrieking,
fantastic fun fair funday Sunday.

It was a
traffic jamming, car stopping, horn blowing,
overheating journey back to Sunbury.

Robert Walker (13)
Feltham Community College

SILENCE

It's so silent, I can hear
a police siren 100 miles away
screeching nee nor, nee nor

It was so peaceful I could hear
my toes squelching in my
crisp white socks

It is so still I can hear
the sun burning away
billions of miles away in space

It's so tranquil I can hear
my eyes moving
around in my head.

It's so very, very quiet!

David Hargreaves (13)
Feltham Community College

DIAMOND POEMS

Light
It opens
With so much love
Darkness is coming to attack
Start to get dark very, very quickly
Until the morning
Break is over
Light is over
Dark.

Milad Mahmoodi (12)
Feltham Community College

LOVE - HATE

Love!
I love your
Short blond hair
Your lovely blue eyes
I begin to know and hate your
Short blond hair
And your horrible blue eyes
I hate you
Hate!

Natasha Fitzwater (11)
Feltham Community College

MY SEASIDE SONG

On our day at the seaside we:
Sun-tanned,
Saw a band,
Played chase,
Won a race,
Sang songs,
Hummed tunes,
Ate ham,
Swam,
All in the first hour.

Then we made a big munch of lunch,
Chased bees,
Washed our knees,
Played catch in sandy dunes,
Bought balloons,
Hummed more tunes,
Saw baboons
(And we *still* hadn't found out how to put up the deck chairs)
We fed the goats,
Rowed some boats,
Then built a sandcastle with a great big moat.

It was a great day, we all agree,
We even got home in time for tea!

Sarah O'Brien (12)
Feltham Community College

ON THE WAY TO CORNWALL

On the way to Cornwall
It was hot, sticky and not very cool
Stuck behind a baby chair
Being cramped was like a rule
When we got to the campsite the sun shone very bright
But when we played bingo
That really did give me a fright
The swimming pool was big and small
That's alright for my brother because he's very tall
The caravan was very nice, a toilet, a shower and two bedrooms
It's good for my mum, no cleaning, no dustpans, no brushes
                                                    and no brooms.

Liam O'Leary (12)
Feltham Community College

IT WAS SO

It was so silent that I could hear
the movement of a slug.

It was so quiet that I could hear
the cat drinking its milk.

It was so calm I could hear
my heart pounding.

It was so peaceful I could hear
the whisper of the butterfly's wings.

It was so still that I could hear the
breathing of air.

Jonathon Collins (12)
Feltham Community College

EXCLUSIONS

I can remember when I got excluded,
It wasn't fair, it wasn't fair,
All I did was skid,
But I really didn't care.

I had a mouse which was two months of age,
Which I put in Jack's colour case,
Once I had broken a rabbit cage,
And the teacher pulled a funny face.

I can remember lunch time,
It was very cool,
Someone threw a piece of slime,
Well, it's better than doing work in school.

I can remember my mates,
And my best friend,
I helped them jam the gates,
Got into trouble in the end.

I can remember my worst subject,
I hated it more than you,
They wouldn't even let me elect,
So I ran into the loo.

I picked a bug from the garden,
Actually it was a wood-louse,
I didn't want to learn,
So that's why I'm in my house.

Anisha Shah (11)
Feltham Community College

HOT COFFEE

Hot,
Coffee,
Is tasty,
With a biscuit,
With a bit of sugar,
Slowly it cools,
Once it's cool,
And stale,
It's
Cold.

Daniel Jackson (11)
Feltham Community College

NIGHT TO LIGHT

Night
it's dark
it's very scary
light starts to open
and out comes
a flash
light

Laurence Hart (11)
Feltham Community College

ANIMAL POEM

An angry ape attacked my army.
Busty bee beat up a beaver.
Curly cat kicked a cow.
Dipsy dog dipped a duck.
Empty elephant ate Ernie's ear.
Fizzy frog felt fried.
Green gorilla got a green dog.
Hungry hippo had hold of Harry's hair.
Ignorant Irene hit an Igloo.
Jumping Jack jumped a baboon.
Killing kangaroo killed Kyle.
Leaping leopard liked Larry.
Monkey Mark made mince with magpies on Monday.
Nutty nit nutted a newt.
Orang-utan owl owled over night.
Percy pig pecked trees.
Quacking queen quacked a duck.
Rich rhinos made a riot.
Silly snakes eat sausages.
Turning tiger turned blue.
Unicorn uses a uniform.
Vultures vote for ventura.
Wacky wolf walks west.
Yorkshire terriers use yachts.
Zebras use a zebra crossing.

Mark Port (12)
Feltham Community College

ANIMAL ALLITERATION POEM

A n angry ant attacked an armadillo
B enny bat brought a brainy buffalo
C rafty cows created cheese
D ick Dastardly's dog died
E normous elephants ruined Europe
F at frogs fell forward
G old gorilla made lovely cakes
H ungry horses hurried home
I nsects in Ibex's igloo
J umping jaguar's car
K ing killed koala king
L ambs leaping long
M ouse's money mayhem
N ewt's now nothing
O ctopus' orange addiction
P refect pigs are polite
Q ueen bee ran quickly
R unning Rodger rabbit
S ting of screaming sounds
T urtle trouble in Toronto
U nicorn underwear is unbelievable
V ulture venom kills
W ombats wobble wherever wanted
Y aks walked yesterday
Z ebra lives in a zoo.

Christopher Munday (12)
Feltham Community College

FALLING

Falling, falling, down into darkness,
  Falling into nothing.
    Darkness, darkness, endless darkness,
      Don't know when it will end.

Peril, peril, peril in darkness,
  Peril at the bottom,
    Quiet, quiet, fall through darkness,
      Mist enshrouds the pit.

Cobwebs, cobwebs, hundreds of millions,
  Through the silken webs I fall.
    Fungi, fungi, covering the walls,
      Nothing to hold on to, I fall on.

But then light, light, at the bottom,
  I may be safe at last.
    Hope, hope, fills my heart,
      As I fall towards the light very fast.

Bump, bump, I hit the mud,
  I see a door in the wall,
    Freedom, freedom, from my fall,
      The endless fall into darkness.

Nikki Williams (12)
Longford Community School

Toothaches, Toothaches

Toothaches, toothaches
a mouth full of pain,
they drive me crazy
in fact, insane!

They always put me
in a really bad mood,
because I can't chew
my yummy food!

My mum said
I've just the ticket,
off to the dentist
we must visit!

The dentist said
'lay on the couch,'
I've got a feeling
I'm about to say ouch!

Oh no, oh no
he has to inject my gum,
'Sit still and be quiet'
said my mum!

When I got home
my teeth no longer hurt,
thanks to the dentist
my old friend Burt!

Sherise Kennelly (12)
Longford Community School

BULL-MASTIFFS

Bull-mastiffs have wrinkly heads,
You get fawns and brindles and reds.
They grow big and strong
And will pull you along,
Unless you train them they'll stray.
They are good guard dogs I'd say,
Efficient, alert through the day -
But God help you at night
If you give them a fright,
You are better off staying away.
Bull-mastiffs have lots of wit,
And mouths full of horrible spit.
It sticks to the telly like white foamy jelly
And glues in your hair like a nit.
We go to dog shows as you've guessed.
Our dogs are the biggest and best.
I hope to win, I confess,
And compete with the best of the rest.

Michael White (11)
Longford Community School

THE BATH

As I stepped into the depths of his warm soapy belly,
The bubbles rose and he covered me with his crashing waves,
As I jumped out,
The hole in the bottom,
Sucked away his life.

Wesley Dack (11)
Longford Community School

MONSTER

There's a monster in my bedroom Mum,
I'll tell you what it's like.

Its head is like a lampshade
that shines brighter than the sun.

Its body is like a giant scaly fish
with fire all around.

Its claws are like a razor-sharp tree
able to split a man in two.

Its teeth are like werewolf fangs
dripping with blood.

I know you don't believe me Mum
but hurry up, it's getting closer,
It's . . . arrrgghh.

Mark Parker (11)
Longford Community School

THE WASHING UP LIQUID BOTTLE

He sits in wait on the empty platform
Silently, silently, he waits for his victim
As his victims fall into the murky depths
He slowly opens his cannon-like head
The victims lie in the water below unsuspecting,
Then he strikes.
A thick green poisonous liquid oozes out.
As the water turns to poison quicker and quicker
The victims' bodies melt away
Leaving only a shiny white skeleton.

Robert Fellowes (11)
Longford Community School

SCHOOL'S OUT

It's time to play,
No more homework, hip hip hooray.
We can go to the park,
Play on the swings.
Stay up late to do our own thing.

A day trip to the seaside,
To paddle in the waves,
Then lie on the sand and soak up the rays.

Six weeks have passed
Our fun comes to an end,
Time to return to school,
To see all our friends.

Sophie Harmer (12)
Longford Community School

THE HOUSE

The house waiting for somebody to devour and close the door
behind him,
As he enters he quickly wipes his feet on the house's tongue,
As he gallops further he enters the stomach that we call the living room,
The stairway looms and looks like the intestine as this person winds
his way through
The central heating system looks very much like the nerves in a human,
The thing that keeps this house going is the pump, which acts
as the heart.

Amandeep Gill (11)
Longford Community School

You!

You!
Your head is like a football.
You!
Your eyes are like torches.
You!
Your ears are like wings.
You!
Your nostril is like a mouse's hole.
You!
Your mouth is like a lump of mud.
You!
Your hand is like a wooden post.
You!
Your legs are like a pencil.

Shahnawaz Umer (13)
Longford Community School

Eleven

If I had been born yesterday
I wouldn't be a pest today
I'd only be one day old
Nothing would have I been told
All I'd do is eat, sleep, and rest all day.

In 364 days I'd be one year old,
There would have been lots I'd been told,
I walk, talk, I even sing,
I'm just about into everything,
I would have been a pest I've been told.

Jacob Clark (11)
Longford Community School

VALENTINE

Here comes the Valentine for me this year,
He is so handsome, so strong and divine,
Do you think he will come to be my dear,
Or will I find out that he is not mine?

Springtime is the time we find new life begins,
We find life abounds in fields and meadows,
Farm hands and workers partake of the inns,
And walk home at night through moonlit shadows.

Valentine, Valentine, won't you be mine?
I dream of the time this will come to be,
Then we will find that our lives will entwine,
Oh Valentine, when will you come to me?

This sonnet it tells of love and our time,
And I hope that I catch my Valentine.

Kirsty Woodbridge (12)
Longford Community School

THE TAXI DRIVER

A brave taxi driver called Clive,
Didn't really know how to drive,
Then he crashed into a truck,
With not much luck,
Because he didn't survive.

Melissa Elsley (11)
Longford Community School

THE UNREQUITED LOVE

She sees him every day,
But cannot speak his name,
She wants to talk to him - but can't,
She is speechless.

Aimlessly she wanders around him,
Trying to get his attention,
Yet he does not notice her,
And her tries remain hopeless.

She tortures herself,
Thinking of him day and night,
Yet he does not realise,
The pain she suffers.

She sees him in the hallway,
His soft blond hair,
His mystical blue eyes,
She wants to call his name.

She is the longing admirer,
The secret love that does not exist,
Yet he does not notice her,
For it is the 'unrequited love'.

Vijal Patel (12)
Longford Community School

THE WIND

He strides slowly, carefully among the leaves
Causing them to rustle.

His long hair whispers at the cheeks on the children in the park
Leaving them rosy-cheeked and apple-faced.

He tiptoes by the tree, and his flowing cape snags on a branch
It sways gently to and fro.

His eyes glint mischievously as he cartwheels through the rosebeds
Scattering petals all over the ground.

He is not afraid - he roars to show who is the king
And he leaps, full of grace, through the air.

He dances around houses, knocking on windows
Daring the brave to face his wrath.

He eventually begins to age and staggers to a tiny corner of the earth
Where he curls up for a long sleep.

And there, he dies
But his spirit is left to roam the land, until it
Is grown into the beast that wind is
And claim his throne once again.

Sarah Tennant (13)
Longford Community School

MY BEST FRIEND

My best friend Jade
Is very kind,
She lends me her things
And I lend her mine.

When I moved to my house
That was when I first saw Jade,
But what was weird
Was how quickly we made friends.

I chose Jade as a friend
Because she's funny and kind,
But if I get a bit angry
She won't mind.

But Jade has one bad point,
It's that Jade gets a bit excited,
But when she gets to where she's going
She is delighted.

Kerry Sparkes (11)
Longford Community School

IMAGINE

Imagine a mouse as big as a house,
Imagine a bee as big as a tree,
Imagine a frog as long as a log,
Imagine a fly as big as the sky,
Imagine a dog as wild as a hog.

Charley Yates (12)
Longford Community School

THE MAN WITH THE SUITCASE

The man with the suitcase,
Is the same man with the briefcase,
He's not got a pretty face,
The man with the suitcase.

He may not be popular,
But he has a favourite Rugrat, Angelica,
And he also loves the custard, Ambrosia,
The man with the suitcase.

He has a mobile phone,
With lots of wicked tones,
He also has wobbly bones,
That silly, silly man with the suitcase.

Leanne Welfare (11)
Longford Community School

JASON'S APPLES

Jason's apples, red and green,
apples like you've never seen,
they're big and small,
it doesn't matter, I like them all.
They're sour and sweet and good to eat,
chewy and crunchy and very munchy
and very, very good for your teeth.
On the tree there's an apple waiting for me.

Jason Keen (11)
Longford Community School

CHOCOLATE FRENZY

It's smooth and creamy and comes in many flavours,
Dark, white or brown, round and straight wafers.
When you see the wrappers you lick your lips,
Thinking of the taste makes you fall to bits.

Eat it solid and cold or drink it down hot,
Either way you eat it, you won't be able to stop.
Coated with caramel and dipped in nuts,
Eat a giant gateau, if you have the guts.

Chocolate flavoured ice-cream tastes the best,
Or chocolate flakes on ice-cream they rest.
Eat it slowly or wash it all down fast,
It goes the quickest when you're trying to make it last.

It fits in your pocket, but don't leave it there long,
On a hot sunny day it will soon start to pong.
So the secret of chocolate is to eat it quick,
But the way you eat it is your choice to pick.

Roxanne Winton (11)
Longford Community School

ANIMALS

A   is for animals, great and small,
N   is for nightingale in the trees,
I   is for insects like moths and bees,
M   is for monkeys high above ground,
A   is for ants scurrying around,
L   is for lions in their dens,
S   is for snakes that sliver around,
        up a tree or underground

Jodie Wells (12)
Longford Community School

FIRE

Red,
Orange
With a hit of yellow,
Equals *fire*.

Oxygen,
Heat,
Air,
Equals *fire*.

Burns,
And
Death,
Equals *fire*.

Fire is dangerous,
Fire is deadly,
Fire is *not* to be messed with!

Jason Bona (11)
Longford Community School

MY BROTHER

As I watch the day go by,
I look at the twinkle in the sky,
And think what would life be,
With you by my side,
I know you're there somewhere looking down on me
I keep a picture by my bed,
And think you should be here instead.

Kylie Sutton (11)
Longford Community School

SEASONS

In the autumn breeze
When the leaves fall off the trees.
Running round
The leaves all rustle on the ground.

In the winter comes the snow,
Over the streams the ice will glow.

Round the corner spring is here,
You can hear the birds' song in your ear.

In the morning the sun comes up early,
As it's summer now the brambles grow curly.
There's blackberries to pick
And ice lollies on a stick.

Kelly Anderson (11)
Longford Community School

SUN

In the morning a baby is born,
Filling the world with happiness and praise
They pray to this king, hoping he will not die.
But their happiness fades. The king is ill.
Is their hope that this king will live?
The king dies peacefully.
The world is filled with sorrow again
Their hearts are broken, never to be repaired.
Will he come again?

Mary Reilly (13)
Longford Community School

MY BEST FRIEND

R eady to give a helping hand, that's my friend.
O n our bikes we cycle all day, that's my friend.
B etter than the best at computers, that's my friend.
E asy to talk to, that's my friend.
R eliable and kind, that's my friend.
T he best friend, a friend can have, that's my friend.

Aaron Fullick (12)
Longford Community School

RAINBOW

R ed as a flame,
A nd as bright as ever.
I ndigo, there's nothing to say about that.
N ow let's carry on!
B rown can be very dull.
O range is alive.
W hite is alarmed.

Elizabeth Franklyn (11)
Longford Community School

KIRSTY

I have a friend called Kirsty,
She's always very thirsty,
She eats her food with honey,
I think it's rather funny,
She keeps it on the knife,
She's done it all her life.

Shannon Deal (13)
Longford Community School

A SAD SONG

Tears trickle down your cheek
for your future looks very bleak.
Darkness forms around your head,
it feels like you are dead.
Lightning splits your heart in two,
your face is covered in a mouldy goo.
You cannot see for you are blind,
away out of this place, you cannot find.
All you see is awful weather,
it seems that you'll be sad forever!

Sara Wood (11)
Longford Community School

TEACHERS AND SCHOOL

We're going to school,
We're out of school,
Playing with our friends is so much cooler than school.

Sometimes we can't go out,
We have horrible homework to do every single day.

All we hear is teachers moaning and groaning about
students every second of the day.

So you know what I mean.

Komal Anwar (11)
Longford Community School

YORKSHIRE TERRIER

I walk up the path, and through my door,
As I have done so many times before.
Then, I am greeted by my best friend,
A Yorkshire terrier with love to spend.
He's black and tan, and oh so sweet,
I am so glad he's there to meet.
We love each other oh so much,
My heart goes out for him to touch.

Vicky Bhyat (12)
Longford Community School

THE SUN, THE MOON AND THE STARS

The sun rides across the sky in her golden chariot,
She pokes her golden fingers through my curtain,
She yawns and wakes in the morning then,
Gallops across the sky to go to bed in the silky
                    black quilt of the night.

The moon smiles in a shadow,
And argues with the sun,
And when he gets angry he commands the seas to crash,
He guards the world at night.

The school of stars
Performs a dance to the moon,
Then circles the Earth
And winks the world to sleep.

Joanna Hossack (11)
Northwood School

WEATHER

The howling tornado,
The crashing tidal wave,
The flashes of lightning,
The continuous rage.

The bang of thunder,
The whistle of the hurricane,
The patter of rain,
Hurricane Dwayne.

People screaming on the beach,
The thud of footsteps
Running to the shelter,
The Tsunami depth.

Thomas Melton (11)
Northwood School

AN OBSCURE STILLNESS

An obscure stillness
Spreading like an illness
In a deep, dark sleep,
No noise
Apart from the sound of rustling leaves.

A big silhouetted tree
Towering over me,
Reaching up to the sky;
The fluttering sounds of bats in flight
Looking for some flesh to bite.

Jennifer Yarrow (11)
Northwood School

CHRISTMAS MORNING

A cold winter's night,
The snow outside a wonderful sight,
The garden wrapped up in a blanket of snow.
Me, my parents, my brothers and co,
The presents safely under the tree,
We were having fun, my family and me.
Soon as it was Christmas morning,
And the day was just dawning,
In the lounge was where we met,
Anxious to see what we could get.
In that room was the tree
With my presents just waiting for me.
I opened, I liked,
I kicked with excitement,
What was inside the red and blue dressing
I will not tell so you will have to keep guessing . . .

Philip J Grehan (11)
Northwood School

A DARK NIGHT

The darkness silently slithered over the world,
Smothering the light with darkness;
The trees came alive,
Their hands scratched the windows of houses,
While the moon stood silently witnessing the nightly goings on.
Shadows danced on the walls,
Stars pierced the blackness of the night sky, sparkling high above;
Rustlings filled the air,
A high-pitched scream came to my ears,
A menacing scarecrow sways in the wind,
And then light prised the darkness away from the Earth, bringing day.

Daniel O'Brien (12)
Northwood School

A DARK NIGHT

There was an eerie silence
as the enormous castle loomed
over them.

The dark murky air whistled around
the troopers as they climbed up the
menacing mountain to their destination.

Shadows lurking around the castle
just longing for their prey.

There was a dim light glowing in the
castle that could hardly be noticed.
The troopers made their way to the light.

An eerie feeling hung in the castle.
In the morning the troopers were
nowhere to be found.

Alice Walsh (11)
Northwood School

FOOTBALL

F   ootball is good, football is bad.
O   n and off the players go,
O   n and on the managers go.
T   he players do what the managers say,
B   ut they let in a goal.
A   ll the players moan.
L   ost again, lost again you bunch of idiots.
L   ast place is ours.

Greg Townsin (11)
Northwood School

A DARK NIGHT

I stare out of the window, my mind as blank as the night itself;
Only a sprinkling of diamond-like stars interrupts the inky
blackness of the night sky.
I gaze out of my window to see a misshapen saucepan-like
constellation, which is The Plough.
The only other light is the moon's glorious luminous beam.

This autumn night feels cold
and leaves crackle and crunch under foot,
no longer warmed by the sun's glow.
The nocturnal animals slowly slide from their daytime hiding places,
emerging only to hide under a blanket of darkness.
Again I stare out of my window;
the night is dissolving as day begins to break.

Alex Baulch (11)
Northwood School

THE SEA

The sea is an angry dog
that howls and bites.

The sea is a vicious bear
that roars and fights.

The sea is an angry child
screaming and kicking its legs.

The sea is a giant,
tall and angry.

The sea is stubborn
and fearsome.

Adrienne Heath (11)
Northwood School

THE FUNFAIR

Wahhoo!
Is the noise coming from the roller-coaster.
The track *roars!*
As the carriage turns the corner.
Bang!
As a ball hits a coconut on the coconut shy.
Wallop!
As someone hits the test your strength machine.
Ting!
As the light reaches the top.
Yeehaa!
Is the shout of a boy on the bucking bronco.
Ha Ha!
Is the noise coming from the clown show.

Splash!
Goes the water on the log flume.
Squelch!
As the people get out of the carriage.
Whoosh!
As the runaway train goes past.
Wow!
As the children get off.
Yay!
As their mum buys them candyfloss.
Fizz!
As they open a can of coke.
Bye!
As they leave to go home.

Angharad Birtles (11)
Northwood School

THE BUS

When I start my journey in the morning
I dread the noisy children,
Who squash me,
Who sit on me,
I dread the slow traffic jams.

The driver crams them on,
I nearly touch the floor,
No one ever talks to me,
Think about that!

With no one ever
Talking to you,
Wouldn't that make you feel lonely?

I do the same journey
Over and over again,
Until,
The end
Of the
Day.

Amy Sawtell (11)
Northwood School

STAR

As I gleam down on the Earth
And start to lose fire as I grow old,
Lighting up the space as I know
Only of darkness and people wishing
Upon me throughout the night.

Dan Fortella (11)
Northwood School

THE SEA

As I run to catch the pebbles,
And the seashells beg and beg me to sing,
So I begin to sing with all my might,
But, then it turns into a mighty laugh as the
                         seaweed starts to tickle me.

I soon get annoyed with all the people,
Jump, jump, jumping on me!
But, as I try to push them off
They always laugh and think it's fun.

Soon night-time falls,
Everyone leaves,
I start to get tired
And wave goodnight to the moon.

Jodie Simmons (11)
Northwood School

NORTHWOOD SCHOOL

Come to school and don't be late,
By train or bus with your best mate.
At 10.50 go out to play
This is the first break of your day.

Next is maths, you've got a test
But teacher knows you'll try your best.
Lastly is art, you're using clay,
In 50 mins you'll have finished your day!

Kayleigh Thomas (11)
Northwood School

THAT'S WHAT THEY SAID

'Your country needs you more than ever now!'
That's what they said!

'We're going to beat the Germans, they won't
know what hit them.'
That's what we said, when we all joined!

'Bye Mum, bye darling, don't worry it
will all be over by Christmas and I'll be
home just you'll see.'
That's what we said when we left home!

'I'll be the first in line, to shoot all the Germans.'
That's what we said on the train!

Bang! Bang! Bang!
That's not what we said!

'Screams, cries, shouts of help, no not me,
please I didn't start it.'
That's what we said!

'Attack.'
That's what they said.

'Ding, dong'.
'Mrs Hampton, telegram . . . sorry Miss.'
That's what they said!

Kelly Whoriskey (11)
Northwood School

THE TREE

I'm stuck in the winter, freezing cold,
Standing here big and bold,
In the autumn my leaves fall off,
And twirl to the ground really soft.

My hands do almost reach the sky,
And that is really high.
My body is round and big,
And my legs dig right into the ground.

At breaktime the children swing on my branches,
Especially that girl, Frances.
They swing and swing until they break,
They just don't understand what a life for a tree is like.

My heart pumps water around my branches,
Heating my trunk up so it's really warm.
The thing is, to humans I'm a dead creature
But I wish my life was more exciting.
People are really a pain in the trunk!

Kimberley Robson (11)
Northwood School

THE WITCH FROM THE WEST

There was a funky witch from the west,
Who had had her magic spells' test,
She got a high score,
Charmed the champagne to pour,
Then she got drunk and laid down to rest.

Philippa Monypenny (11)
Northwood School

THE DOLPHIN

The dolphin sings a lullaby to you,
It goes through
The water like a knife shredding paper.
Gentle, loving, caring
Is the dolphin.

I am a
Submarine voyaging the oceans hidden worlds,
A killer running from a band of raging cops,
But all that is, is imagination
Says the dolphin.

The dolphin
Is a trapeze artist
Flying through a world of doom.
Never frightened is the dolphin
That's what the dolphin says.

Toni Emma Metcalf (11)
Northwood School

THE ANT

I walked down a path one day,
And I saw a little ant, and I thought I heard him say,
'Please could you stop your stamping on the ground,
As we would like our little nest to be safe and sound.'

'Every day I go and look for food,
But all you humans seem to be in a foul mood,
You almost step on me,
Can't your see?
Please don't step on me.'

Devan Pankhania (11)
Northwood School

OLD WOMEN

Scars and bruises were like
Warnings and signs of a slow and
Painful death.
What had happened to her in the past?
Nobody knows . . .

A haunting face looks back at you,
Telling you what's right from wrong.
The attitude on her face is like a
Reflection of her past,
Reminding you what could happen to
You if you don't look after yourself.

Her lips were dark as the starless
Midnight sky spreading over the innocent earth.
Sympathy is what you feel for the old and
Battered women.
Where had she come from?
Who was she?
Nobody knows . . .

Ushma Mistry (11)
Northwood School

LAMP POST

I am
the tall lamp post,
8ft high, 50 inches wide.
I shine the light every day.

The kids always come
and start kicking me but
I just don't take any notice.

I stay up every day
watching the cars go by,
while they are going they usually
throw rubbish at me from the carrrrr.

Now it's time to go because
I have been cut down.
I had a wonderful life,
Now it's gone,
So I will see you in heaven.

Abdul Malik (11)
Northwood School

THE LAMP POST SONG

I am a lamp post,
I'm the best,
I shed some light on my street.
As people walk by at night
They never walk in fright,
'Cos they know that they're safe with me.

In the daytime I don't shine,
The sun does my job and thinks he's so fine.
As night has come I can do my job,
And I'll sometimes see a space pod,
For I live next to NASA.

Every night some people come by,
And they thank me for the light,
If I could talk I'd love to say, Hi to them,
And when they come home I'd love to say, Goodnight.

Mohammed Basma (12)
Northwood School

THE SEA

The sea is a growling wolf,
It howls whilst coming up the beach
looking for something nice to eat.
It is very fierce but can be calm,
This particular wolf goes on for yards.

The sea is a horrid bear,
It keeps on growling all night long,
It keeps on growling all day long.
Inside his stomach you will see
all the fish from the big blue sea.

The sea is a fierce tiger
biting on your feet
when people come in
to get out of the blistering heat.

Kate Balkin (11)
Northwood School

COUNTRY SETTING

The grass is greener than a cucumber,
The tractors make more noise than a crash of thunder,
The hills are higher than the tallest school,
There are more flowers than all the people in the world times six,
The streams are cleaner than the cleanest water,
The cottages with thatched roofs are like a hot dog with a bun,
The air is fresher than freezing water,
The animals dance and play like children in a playground,
The moors are as long as the hours in a week,
The trees are taller than Mount Everest,
The isolated village is like a diamond.

Luke Colwill (11)
Northwood School

I LIKE NOISE

I like noise in the morning.
The beep, beep of the alarm clock.
The bathroom door slamming.
The creak of the stairs.
The squeak of a knife.
The smash of a plate.
The crackle of cereal.
The crunch of toast.
The front door crashing.
The birds tweeting.
The swish of traffic.
I like noise.

Nicholas Borton (11)
Northwood School

UNTIL I SAW THE SEA

Until I saw the sea
I did not know
that sunlight
could shimmer on the sea.

I never knew
that waves
could swallow up rocks.

Nor
did I know before
that crabs walk sideways
along the shore.

Jamie-Lee Lover (11)
Northwood School

THE CARP SONG

I just sit there waiting for prey,
Bored on the bottom of the bed, not moving a muscle.
Then I saw a fisherman coming to the edge of the river.
I thought *'yum'* breakfast at last, was this maggots on toast?
He set up his fishing rod and he put the maggot on the line,
I was still sitting there.
He cast and in came the maggot.
I just sat there for a little while,
Then I attacked the maggot as hard as I could.
I thought, *'he ha'* fisherman you're coming in,
We were there for ten minutes and I was getting weaker and weaker,
But then I gave it a mighty tug,
Yes I'd won again.

Lee Collum (11)
Northwood School

THE SHEEPDOG

All day I must chase sheep,
I never get a rest,
I am always very thirsty,
And the sheep think they're the best.

I never get a drink,
I'm not allowed in the house
'Cause they say I'm dirty
And they say I always stink.

I'm always getting shouted at.
I do get very hot,
All I want is a day of rest,
A day when I'm the best.

Holly Frost (12)
Northwood School

I Am What I Am

I am what I am,
The most courageous boy.

I am what I am,
The most fast boy.

I am what I am,
The most sensitive boy.

I am what I am,
The most considerate boy.

I am what I am,
The most loving boy.

I am what I am,
The most annoying boy!
(But only to my sister).

Manish Kerai (11)
Preston Manor High School

Myself!

Hi! My name is Himesh Tailor,
I like playing golf,
But I'd rather play with an energetic fork.
I like being at school,
But it's better in a swimming pool.
My name is Himesh,
The happiest boy on Earth, *so there.*

Himesh Tailor (11)
Preston Manor High School

A POEM ABOUT ME

A bout me.

P reston Manor is my school,
O nly last year I was in year 6,
E xcept now I'm in year 7.
M y hobbies are singing and dancing.

A cting is my ambition.
B rown hair, brown eyes,
O rdinary but
U nique, and full of surprise.
T ala is my name.

M y favourite sport is swimming,
E ducation is my aim.

Tala Holmes-Gouveia (11)
Preston Manor High School

A POEM ABOUT ME

Sports do not hold my interest,
School's alright,
Stationery's simply the best.

My favourite subject is art,
Geography's the worst,
English touches my heart.

God is the one who I believe in,
I don't believe in tooth fairies,
My sense of smell disappears as I sniff the bin.

Jharna Bhatia (11)
Preston Manor High School

ABOUT ME

I am tall,
I like playing with a ball.

I wear a blue coat
and I like playing with a boat.

My favourite colour is blue
and bubblegum is what I like to chew.

I like toy cars
and I like eating chocolate bars.

I like bicycle rides
and I like going down slides.

Peter Lewinson (11)
Preston Manor High School

MY POEM

I'm really interested in sports,
My favourite sports are football and cricket,
I'm also good at other sports.

When I'm not in a good mood
I get very annoyed and I get moody.
I'm very energetic if I want to be,
I'm very energetic if I'm playing sports.

I like watching wrestling,
WCW and WWF are my favourite.
That's me Junaid.

Junaid Manzoor (11)
Preston Manor High School

SLAVERY

Why do these white men
Judge us black people
By the colour of our skin?

We are not the ones
Who are committing
The sins.

Is it because we are
Different from you?
Is it because we're black
Not white like you?

We are not animals,
But human beings.
You think white is superior,
We are like dirt to you.

You whip us like the horses
You ride,
Why do you do this?
Don't you think we have pride?

Busy as bumblebees,
We work all day,
In the hot baking sun,
Picking cotton 'till we're done.

Simone Austin (12)
Preston Manor High School

I'M THE VICTIM

I'm the victim,
They come to look for me.
Now they have me,
Me the victim.

I'm the victim.
I get pushed and kicked
As the rest stare and laugh.
Me the victim.

I'm the victim
With a face covered in blood.
I can't recognise myself,
Me the victim.

I'm the victim,
I can't take any more,
I want to die.
Me the victim.

Heemali Patel (13)
Preston Manor High School

SLAVERY

Slaves had to work all day,
Some even tried to run away,
If they did, they still got caught.
They could not read or write, they didn't get taught,
Even if they did all the work they still got a beating.

Mili Patel (12)
Preston Manor High School

FROM VICTIM TO VICTOR

Me the victim . . .
Do I rage in anger?
Do I have feelings?
Me the victim . . .

Me the victim . . .
Can I overcome it?
Will I overcome it?
Me the victim . . .

Me the victim . . .
I will stand up to him.
I have to defeat him.
Me the victor . . .

Me the victim . . .
Will you defeat him?
Will you be a victor?
Me the victor . . .

Shima Parbat (13)
Preston Manor High School

SLAVERY

Slaves had to work all day,
They had to work every day,
Slaves had to work hard or they got beaten,
And when they got beaten they had to work faster
And even harder and make food so it gets eaten.
Slavery is bad and it's sad.

Nimisha Thakor (12)
Preston Manor High School

WHAT SHOULD I DO?

I am always the person they pick on,
I hate coming to school,
My teachers don't pay attention,
What should I do?

They hit me and call me names,
My friends are scared too,
They do tell the teacher but
What should I do?

I will not take it any more,
My head is spinning around,
I don't want to live any more,
What should I do?

Hershika Kerai (13)
Preston Manor High School

PAIN

Whipped, hit every day,
Slavery is very unfair I say.
Just because the colour of your skin
You're not to go where you want.
You should always do your chores,
You do what they want for no money.
And if you try to run away because you feel sad
They will send a catcher after you.
And if they catch you, you will be badly beaten.

Eugene Anderson (13)
Preston Manor High School

SLAVES

Slaves have to wake up
before dawn cracks,
Or they'll get cat-o'-nine-tails
on their backs.
They have to work
so hard each day.
They are whipped
if they don't do what Massa say.
The field hand slaves
pick cotton bushes,
The household slaves
wash all the dishes.
Some slaves have stamina
to pick cotton bushes all day long,
But others get whipped,
they cry and they mourn.
The white man say
to the black man, Nigger,
He makes the weight
of cotton bags bigger.
There is a land
called Canada,
Slavery is . . .
banned there.

Princess Omonira (12)
Preston Manor High School

SLAVERY

Slaves are people who are taken away
To work for masters the live long day.

They have no break and if they slack
They feel a whip upon their backs.

They take abuse and they get beatings,
They get called names with racist meanings.

If the slaves try to escape,
They would be taken back in chains.

Then get whipped until they bleed,
Never again would they try to leave.

The slave masters were very mean,
They would not give slaves a proper meal.

Most of the slaves were very weak,
But had to pick cotton in the fields.

They lived in cabins on plantations,
And in families there were many separations.

No matter how hard we may try
We just cannot understand why,

So many people in those days
Could be so cruel to all those slaves.

Slaves are people who are taken away
To work for masters the live long day.

Caprisha Pennant (12)
Preston Manor High School

REMEMBERING

Beaten, kicked, bruised and hurt,
I sit in front of the mirror,
Seeing my reflection,
Remembering that day
I got bullied.

Sitting alone
In the playground,
Hearing laughter, giggles and happiness,
But me, scared and frightened,
Hoping for him not to come.

Praying for me not to be here,
Wishing for me to die,
Why does he pick on me?
Why am I his victim?
Too many questions, not enough answers.

No one can help me,
My friends are all scared,
My teachers don't know,
And my parents don't care,
Who can help me now?

I feel so miserable,
I feel so pathetic,
Why can't I stand up to him
On my own two feet?
When does this feeling go away?

Beaten, kicked, bruised and hurt,
I sit in front of the mirror,
Seeing my reflection,
Remembering the day I got bullied.

Geeta Patel (13)
Preston Manor High School

MY BULLYING PROBLEM

What makes me do it?
Why do I do it?
Why do I bully all day?

What have they done to me?
Why do I bully them?
Is it just for fun?

What is that voice, inside me saying?
Why does it tell me to do these things?
Or is it just me?

Why can't I stop?
What is the reason?
Someone help me please!

Bhirel Patel (13)
Preston Manor High School

BULLIES

Bullies are foolish,
They pick on little kids.
They don't think when they bully.
Just wait till they get bullied,
They will then feel pain
Just like they caused
When bullying other people.

Shiraz Akhtar (13)
Preston Manor High School

WHY?

Why?
Why do I get bullied?
Why do they bully?

They come after me
After revenge and grief
They cause me stress
They make me scared

Why?
Why do I get bullied?
Why do they get bullied?
Why do they bully?
Why? Why? Why?

I get terrified
I get scared
What's round the corner?
I wonder
We wonder
They wonder

Why? Why? Why?

Bijal Tailor (13)
Preston Manor High School

FREEDOM

F   reedom feet to run to Canada
E   very night you follow the North Star
E   ven though the way is tough
T   ake a chance and hold on to freedom.

Heena Pindoria (12)
Preston Manor High School

THE BULLY

He looks around for me
He spots me
He hates me
Because I am short.

He wants my lunch
He wants my money
He wants me to do his homework
I try to escape

He sees me
He is now ready
He wants me to get hurt
Now I feel the pain.

Michael Etsey Jnr (13)
Preston Manor High School

MOEEN

Moeen is my name,
and being naughty
is my game.
I love to be a pest,
and make lots of mess.
I don't always pass my test
but always try my best.
This doesn't make me sad,
although it makes my mum mad.

Moeen Khan (11)
Preston Manor High School

VICTIM

Why do bullies come after me?
All bullies want to pick on me.
All bullies want to hurt me.
All bullies want to harm me.

Why do bullies come after me?
All bullies want to scare me.
All bullies want to frighten me.
All bullies want money from me.

Why do bullies come after me?
They're all the same.
They're mean.
They're scary.
They're feisty
Why do all bullies do the same?

Sofia Sheikh (13)
Preston Manor High School

BULLIES

Why do I get bullied?
Maybe it is my colour
Why do I get bullied?
Maybe it is what I wear.
Why do I get bullied?
Maybe it is because I'm fat.
Why do I get bullied?
Maybe it is because I am skinny.
Why do I get bullied?
Maybe it is because of what I am.

Ashok Varsani (13)
Preston Manor High School

HOW IT FEELS

Being bullied makes me feel like . . .
Hiding away in a corner
Shutting myself out of the mean, scary world
Going to sleep and never waking up
Pretending that it's a nightmare.
Why does he pick on me?

Being bullied makes me feel like . . .
Shouting out my feelings but then again
Trapping them inside me.
I feel like doing the same to them
Crying all night
Am I really that evil?

I don't need to feel like this
I can find peace
I can go to sleep and never wake up
All I ever wanted was to be their friend.
There's always life after death.

Dipika Vagjiani (13)
Preston Manor High School

UNDERGROUND TO CANADA

F   rightened to escape but finally I reached Canada
R   eacted happily when I got there
E   ncourages others to come with me
E   ncouraged others to come with me
D   esperate for money and for food
O   h I hope the Lord can hear my prayers
M   emories of the others who I left behind
     but I can only hope they will join me soon.

Cherrelle Francis (12)
Preston Manor High School

YOU THINK YOU'RE TOO NICE!

You think you're too nice,
That is why I bully you.
You go on like you're clever
I can be clever too.

You think you're too nice,
That is why I call you names.
You try to ignore me
By playing silly games.

You think you're too nice,
Trying to suck up to the teachers.
We all know that you are Miss' pet.
Well, let me tell you something,
That is the furthest you will get.

You think you're too nice.
Where's my money?
This is no laughing matter.
It is not funny.

You think you're too nice.
Where's my lunch today?
You know, without it you're gonna pay.

Kanika Royer (13)
Preston Manor High School

THE VICTIM

I see him walk, his shadow creeping on me,
There I am walking alone, all in one,
As I walk I wonder why me?
Why me?
Why me?

As he follows, I try to hide,
But he finds me and he does the bully thing,
So I am the victim and he's the bully.

Anil Patel (13)
Preston Manor High School

ME, THE BULLY

I sneak about in the playground,
Who will it be today?
When I find my victim guess what I do,
I punch them,
I kick them,
Until they say 'Mercy.'
But I don't stop,
I take all their money instead of their life,
When the teacher comes that's when I run,
But it's too late! What should I do?

Me, The Victim

Just because you're fat,
If you wear a hat,
They always do it, it's not fair,
My mum is a lollipop lady,
That's real cool to me,
The bully always says to me 'Your mum's sad.'
Which makes me feel so bad,
They hit me,
They punch me,
What can I do?
If they don't stop,
My life is just over now!

Ann Marie Morrison (13)
Preston Manor High School

VICTIM

Bullies, bullies
I hate bullies.
They call me names
Names which make me feel miserable
So miserable that I feel like killing myself.

Bullies, bullies
Nobody can help me
Not my friends, parents or my teachers
I feel like killing them.

Bullies, bullies
I sneak around the playground but they still find me.
There's nowhere to run, there's nowhere to hide
they take my money.
They hit me if I don't do what they tell me to do.

Bullies, bullies
I just hate bullies.

Mansha Varsani (13)
Preston Manor High School

SHE . . .

She who sits next to me,
is always drinking tea.
She has this little flea,
which jumps around on her knee.
The flea is cunning and smiles with glee.
She is a bit silly,
but people say she is as pretty as a lily.
She who sits next to me
will always be drinking tea.

Reena Patel (11)
Preston Manor High School

GROWING UP

When you grow up you become mature,
You never makes jokes or do any funny things.
You end up watching the news,
You don't wear trainers, only shoes.
You never splash out with your money,
You're very tight and stingy.
You always go to shops like C&A and Marks & Spencer,
When I grow up I'm never going to do these things.
When I grow up I'm . . .
Going to be a comedian.
I'm going to buy trainers and caps that cost a lot of money,
I'm going to go to shops like GAP and JD sports only.
I'll never watch the news as long as I'm still young.

Manesh Mistry (12)
Preston Manor High School

BULLIES

I see them walking around
Talking about who they beat up
Showing off like they just don't care
No one knows what these bullies think
No one knows how these victims feel
After these bullies have beaten them up.

They are standing everywhere
Seeing who their next victim is
Laughing and joking
While their victims just sit down and cry
After they beat up one person
They look again for another victim.

Rajesh Jeshani (13)
Preston Manor High School

KICK HIM IN!

I walked around the corner
I saw him,
I had to do something,
Or I would have been thought
Of as a softy.
All my friends started on me.
'Go on! Now's your chance!
Kick him in!'

I went over to him.
He saw me.
He knew I was going to
Do something
So he turned and walked away
From me.
I could see him shivering
But it really wasn't that cold.
I couldn't think of what to
Do to him
Against the wall.
'Give me all your money!'
'No,' he said,
Dropping his bag.
I punched him in the stomach.
I looked at the boys, smiling.
They were pleased.
'Pick up his bag!'
Throw it!' They said.
I picked it up.
I told him to give me his money
Or I would throw his bag away
Into the grotty bin.
'All right, all right,' he said.
He gave me his money, crying.

But still being watched by
The boys,
I threw his bag away.

Then I ran back.
The boys congratulated me;
Slapped me on the back and
All that.
I felt good,
But deep inside,
I knew it
Was wrong.

Ayaaz Esmail (13)
Preston Manor High School

VICTIM

Why me? Why me?
Why do people bully me?
I feel helpless and fearful
I am scared and worried
That tomorrow the bully will strike again

Why me? Why?
Why does he hate me?
Every morning I hide from the bully
He beats me and mocks me
He kicks me and punches me

Why me? Why me?
Why do I get bullied?
I get upset and scared
I feel pathetic and lonely
I try to shout for help
But nobody hears my cries.

Shalin Shah (13)
Preston Manor High School

WHO AM I?

Who am I?
I am Falguni,
I'm the one with the long, black hair.
Who am I?
I am Falguni,
I'm the one who's loving and exciting,
joyful and fun.
Who am I?
I am Falguni,
I'm the one who loves playing netball,
and the favourite subject has to be art!
You know who I am,
Of course it's Falguni,
It has to be the one and only nutter!
I am always there for everyone,
helping them out in their problems.
My friends think of me to be trusting
and so much more!

Falguni Upadhyaya (11)
Preston Manor High School

AUTUMN

In autumn you can hear the
Drip drip sounds of the rain.
As you walk, the leaves blow,
They make a crunch sound
When you walk on them.
Conkers fall on your head,
Misty mornings start the day,
Every day is the same cold day,
As the days get shorter and shorter.

Sabina Nazir (12)
Preston Manor High School

I HAVE A DREAM

I have a dream to see the world
of freedom to know the people
on the other side.

I have a dream of not being whipped
to feel the joy of not being hit.

I have a dream of having proper
food, to not have leftovers and crumbs too.

I have a dream to meet other people who
are not cruel and very hateful.

I have a dream to see my family,
I hope Mammy and Sally will remember me.

I have a dream of not working all day
So I can go and play all day.

I have a dream to go to Canada and
see the adventure ahead.

I have a dream!

Priti Sodha (12)
Preston Manor High School

POEMS ABOUT ME

J   aymini is my name but everyone calls me Jay
A   lways think of myself as a singer
Y   o-yo's are my game, they don't give me shame
M   y ambition is to be a pop star and sweep through the halls of fame
I   n the house I do nothing but sing
N   ight or day
I   try to stay in everyone's good books every day.

Jaymini Naran (11)
Preston Manor High School

ESCAPING TO THE PROMISED LAND

We were all captured from Africa,
tricked and whipped by white Americans.
'Go and pick cotton in the cotton fields,'
the Massa say.
But we can only think about freedom.

On our Massa's plantation,
we work from dawn till dusk.
We work on days with the hot blazing sun beating down
And we work on cold and rainy days.
But we can only thing about freedom.

'Why aren't you slaves workin'?'
We always hear our Massa say,
and then comes the sounds of the whip.
It's hard for us bear
But we can only think about freedom.

'We can't live in such labouring conditions,
we know our rights.' Us slaves suggest.
There is a Promised Land called Canada.
It could be difficult to get there.
But we can only think about freedom.

Us slaves plan our escape to the Promised Land.
It's a place where you can't be owned.
We've heard it's far from the plantation,
even further for the crippled and disabled.
But we can only think about freedom.

As we are on the run for freedom,
we hear the barking of the bloodhounds sent for us.
The hounds are close behind us,
even though the Promised Land is not far now.
But we can only think about freedom.

As we cross the border of Canada,
we know we are free.
No more being owned by a person.
We get the chance to stand up on our own two feet,
But now, we now can on think about . . . *happiness.*

Dunston Laurence Walker (12)
Preston Manor High School

COLD IN THE CORNER

Cold in the corner,
I dread to see the birth of another day,
Another day of cotton picking,
Another day of whips slicing through my skin,
Another day of fearfully looking into
my Massa's heartless, evil eyes.

Many say the white man is evil,
But I know it ain't true,
Cause my pappy told me of a land called Canada
Where the blacks and whites stand together.

I know I can't get there,
I know there's no hope for me,
Cause my Massa's too tight on security.

So I sit there cold in the corner,
Wishing I was with my family,
I sit there cold in the corner,
Hoping for the end,
My end to come.

Admas Haile (13)
Preston Manor High School

THE BULLY

There was a silly little boy called Hairy
His whole family was scary
He was fat and chubby
His eyes were bib and Larry
He was small and thick.

At break we punched him in the eye
We said 'Don't cry, dry your eye, look up in the sky.'
Then the bird did a plop in his eye
Everybody started to laugh
And he started to cry.

At lunch we took his money
We told him to eat this honey bunny
We thought it was funny
He told the teacher to give us detention
So the next day we killed him
Then we threw him in the sewer.

Azizi Foster & Mantas Roderys (13)
Preston Manor High School

MY TYPICAL DAY

N   o geography for me, I hate it but
A   rt is the one I love
B   ut maybe sometimes it's too much, I need a cut
E   ventually I'll take a break and sit
E   specially after running from my brother, the big bully
L   ater on I'll go hang out with some friends, rollerblading
A   nd at the end of the day I take a break from the big bad bully.

Nabeela Yusuf (11)
Preston Manor High School

THE RUNAWAY SLAVE

I am a runaway slave
    I hid in a cave.
I ran away because of the whip
    made of leather
And now there's lots of bad weather
    I was hurt.
Just then I met a boy called Kurt
    I was wounded with blood.
Just then the river caused a flood.
    I followed the North Star.
The journey was quite far
    I went on a cart,
The black driver was quite smart.

Dax Patel (12)
Preston Manor High School

GROWING UP

G   rowing up what a pain
    it drives me very insane
R   emember me
    when I was three
O   h what fun I had
    when I was four
W ater was what I liked
    when I was five
I   was naughty
    when I was six
N   ever mind what I did
    when I was seven
G   rowing up what a pain
    drives me very insane.

Nisha Patel (12)
Preston Manor High School

SLAVERY

Bought and sold like a pig,
Getting beatings, it just takes the mick.
Helpless and poor.
Freedom is a word no more.

Picking the cotton with your hunched up back.
Carrying your life in one paper sack.
Slavery! Why not escape?
Because the Massa will come and beat
you with a rake.

Work and work until you can't no more.
Collect cotton until your back is sore.

There is a land where people are free.
It's called Canada and is a land safe
from Massas and . . . *slavery!*

Hina Gohil (12)
Preston Manor High School

HIM

His eyes shone like sunshine on ice,
His thoughts thinking about nice things
Like snow, fishing or hypothermia - a thing not so nice.
As he walks through the shivering night,
He looks up to the moon which gives a foggy light.

His heart as cold as stone,
His mind hiding secrets never to be known.
As the light icicles of snow fall to the ground,
He wonders if his body will ever be found.

Aishah Khan (12)
Preston Manor High School

APOLOGISE?

It was the new kid,
Yes, it was one of those,
I don't know why I did it,
I guess it made me grow,
Grow into a bigger person,
So I can face my fears,
The hatred of my father
The inconsiderate pain he gave to me.

Oh, why did he do this?
Oh, why was it me?

The violence he released on me,
The pain, the hurt, the sorrow,
I'm not completely sorry,
But I know the pain it leaves,
You think to yourself,
How dare he do this to me?

I know what the new kid's thinking,
I know he must be annoyed with me,
I don't want to say 'Sorry,'
'Cos that's humiliating to me.

So after I finish mistreating him,
I just go home and cry,
Then it's my turn,
To be a victim of my father's crime!

Marlene McFarlane (13)
Preston Manor High School

THE BULLY

I loathe everyone,
I hate them all
I get so much pleasure
By making people depressed
And making them cry

They were mocking me
They deserved what they got
They all feared me
I had to get violent
To keep up my reputation

All of them hid
All were scared
All knew about my power
I had to inflict pain
Upon helpless victims.

I just wished they liked me
I just want friends
I don't want to hurt people
I am not proud of what I do
All I want is for people to get to know me.

Anish Shah (13)
Preston Manor High School

SOMETHING ABOUT ME

P   ooja is my name
O   r people call me Pooj
O   h, but only my close friends are allowed
J   ust be careful what you say
A   nd you will make my perfect day!

Pooja Patel (11)
Preston Manor High School

WHY ME?

Why me? Why me?
What is it he hates
So much about me?
I'm gonna fight back
One of these days.

I can't take it any more
'Help,' I scream
As he beats me repeatedly
'Help, help, help . . . '
No one comes to my rescue.

I feel invisible, 'cos no one cares
I'm scared to walk out my front door
I feel raped of my freedom
Tortured, abandoned, destroyed,
Threatened, terrified, tearful . . .

I have to tell someone
But no one listens
I feel humiliated, depressed
I feel he's snatched my pride
My dignity dissolved
In this vicious circle
It's a mystery to me.

Why me? Why me?
Is he forced to harass me?
Is it hatred or fear?
Why me? Why me?

Zalika Dale (13)
Preston Manor High School

ADULTHOOD

After all those years of having fun it's finally time to grow up,
Days, months, years all just flew by,
Up on my feet ready to face the future,
Little things I just put behind me such as laziness, throwing
tantrums, that's also a part of growing up,
Tough life isn't it, one minute you're having fun and the next
you're too grown up to even do that,
Hence the word 'puberty' it's here where you start to hate
the part of growing up (you know what I mean),
Over the moon about fit boys,
Over the years we start to grow a sense of style and taste,
Day in day out, maturity and growing is what you've got to
think about
I've thought about it and I've decided that I'm going to
Grow up!

Sadia Esmail (12)
Preston Manor High School

MY POEM

I dream I am a billionaire
I dream I spend all my money on cars and sweets
I dream I have a great house with lots of computer games to play with
I dream I can go up to space and see the moon
I dream I am a stunt man who flies through the air on a motorbike
I dream that the world is made of food so you don't go hungry again
I dream that I am a director of the greatest film ever made
I dream I can slam dunk like Michael Jordan
And I also dream I am the greatest poet in the world.

Andrew Watts (11)
Preston Manor High School

GROWING UP

The trouble with growing up,
is no one seems to believe you,
when you do something good or bad,
they still need to talk to you.
Your parents like you being good,
but when you're bad they never understand
your reasons, speeches and explanations too.
None of those talks ever seem to help you,
why as twelve year olds do we try,
to be good every day, oh why oh why?
Growing up and going to secondary school
can sometimes be stressful and they say 'School rules.'

The shame of trying new things with your body
and listening to old groups like Shawaddywaddy.

Aaron Campbell (12)
Preston Manor High School

SCHOOL'S OUT

School's out
Run about.

Boys and girls full of joy
Teachers shouting 'Oh boy!'

Children running for the bus
Grannies shouting 'All that fuss!'

School's out
No one about.

Playground quiet as a mouse
Children shouting in their house.

Kinna Patel (11)
Preston Manor High School

BEING TWELVE

Being twelve is not easy,
you're not a baby,
you're not an adult,
but you *are* stuck in the middle!

Being twelve is annoying,
when you go to the cinema,
the films you want to watch, you can't
and the films you can watch you don't want to.

Being twelve is a pain,
You know you're mature for your age,
but for some reason no one else seems to think so!

Being twelve is a bore
and you can't wait until your thirteenth birthday.
To sum it up . . .
            Being twelve is not fair!

Fasiha Rainaa Malik (12)
Preston Manor High School

PROBLEMS

Problems, problems, problems,
Why? Because we are worried
about something,
or someone.

What problems do you have?
You should leave your
problems behind and look
forward to tomorrow.

My problems?
You ask,
I have many.
Will I do well in school?
What is after death?
When will I die?

Do whatever you enjoy in life
because you are hearing it
from me.
Life is short.
I have many things,
still to see in life.

Miran Shah (12)
Preston Manor High School

GROWING UP

Growing up can be difficult,
Experiencing different things,
                        Problems are on
                        Their minds,
Such as looks and health,
Parents trying to deal,
                        With spending too
                        Much money,
On their children's
Fashionable clothes,
                        Teenagers always,
                        Have to have,
The latest shoes,
Or the latest hairstyles,
                        That's why it's difficult
                        Growing up.

Shareen Safah Ali (12)
Preston Manor High School

I HAVE A DREAM

I have a dream,
That there will be peace
And I shall wear a golden fleece,
As I give the people a tour,
Of something we called war,
Which was unjust,
But we must -
Forget . . .
What we regret . . .
All those lives
Stabbed by knives,
War would be kicked out the door
And racism will be no more.

Mohamed El-Ali (11)
Preston Manor High School

SECRET ADMIRER

I know we've had some bumps in the past
But I'm sure my love for you will last
I've admired you every single day
From the start of the month of May
I talk about you to my friends
And the conversation never ends
I dream about you in the night
And you'll never ever leave my sight
Sorry, I must end my poem here
For the coming of night is very near.
                Sweet dreams!

Kavya Jethwa (13)
Preston Manor High School

EXAMS

Something that happens in every child's life
Is worrying about their exams.
They revise day and night
Hoping to get a good grade.
But when the test arrives
They start to panic,
They do not know what to do.
They see the time ticking away
And pupils scribbling away answers.
Finally they know what to do
They are about to write down an answer
But disturbed by the teacher
Who says:
'Put down your pens!'
The time is up.

You have just failed.

Neel Valera (12)
Preston Manor High School

BULLYING

Being a victim is humiliating,
I'm bewildered and mystified by the abuse.
They pick their targets out at random,
And when they're done, we feel abandoned.

I come in the next day with another bruise,
But they don't care, they want me to lose.
They grab me, kick me, punch my face,
And in the end I feel disgraced.

Rekha Gohil (13)
Preston Manor High School

GROWING UP

Growing up is such a pain,
I'm your host Dilip Patel
once again,
I get up at 6.30 in the morning
and go to school tired and yawning,
the lessons are so boring.
I'd rather be in bed where it is
warm, than outside where
the clouds are booming.
When I get home from school
I have tons of homework to do
which gets on my nerves,
but there's nothing more
annoying until my sister's
friends come over.
They talk and chat
about someone who's really fat.
When it's time to go to sleep
I rest my head and my feet
knowing this day will occur the next day.

Dilip Patel (12)
Preston Manor High School

CRICKET MADNESS

Speed bowling
Massive sixes,
storming runs
Bails falling
shouting madly
'How's that!'

Bhavik J Patel (12)
Preston Manor High School

THE DRAGON

Old dragon,
Used for fire,
Are you a myth I don't know?
Your huge body scares everyone,
Like an elephant's foot you can stomp on us,
Your mighty mouth blows fire,
Like a bomb can be able to destroy everything,
Your mighty colour red,
Shows pride plus danger,
You were used for war,
Never shown to peace,
Like an old shoe used,
But your story will still live on,
Even in the weakest of hour,
A kind creature set to evil,
I still believe in you.

Shavini Wijesuriya (11)
Preston Manor High School

BULLYING

I don't know why they do it
It scares me to death
I want them to stop
But they don't
They come up in gangs
Push me around
They're big and mean
No one can help
I don't know what to do now!

Chandni Odedra (13)
Preston Manor High School

BULLIES

I am stressed to the limit,
I have to let it all out,
All the frustration,
All the anger,

I have to let it all out,
But to whom can I go?
I've stayed in darkness,
Nowhere to go.

I have to break free,
I have to get away,
But the question to ask is,
How, when and where?

Amit Patel (13)
Preston Manor High School

GROWING UP

I really hated growing up
The toothless grin
My crud luck

I hated my school
The teachers were cruel
All they did was smoke and drool

I was short
And stupid
And I believed in Santa Claus

He was an imaginary fraud!

Salman Chaudhry (12)
Preston Manor High School

GROWING UP

Growing up can be a pain
There are lots of worries going on
Parents might say
'You can't wear that, your skirt's too short'
Or
'No way that lipstick is too dark.'
Parents don't know what's in fashion these days.

Growing up can be a pain
You must look perfect when you go out
New hairstyles every day
New clothes every day.
You need to cover the spots
Where you don't want them to grow
To make people notice you.

Growing up can be a pain
You must look like a model
Not that fat or not that thin
You must be somewhere in the middle.

Growing up can be a pain
You need a good grade
To get into a good college
And make your parents proud.

That's why growing up can be
A pain!

Dhrupti Patel (12)
Preston Manor High School

MOVEMENT

The movement of his feet,
The skipping down the street,
The rhythm of the beat
Sounds really sweet.

The way he sways his body,
The air flying through his hair,
The twitch of his neck
Makes him shiver like a pear.

The way his legs stride from side to side,
The way his arms move in time with his legs
And this is where it ends
I've really got to go, see you tomorrow,
Ciao, got to go!

David Joseph (11)
Preston Manor High School

I RAN

I was walking down the corridor
When I saw a gang of bullies
I hated them so much
So I thought I should run
I ran as quick as I could
They ran after me
They thought it was funny
They started to bully me
I had tears running down my eyes
So many lies.

Shazia Sama (13)
Preston Manor High School

WHAT IS A MILLENNIUM?

What is a millennium?
A period of a thousand years,
A time for special change.
New discoveries, new technology,
A brand new age.

New people every day,
Different places, different times,
Different stories, different books,
Different poems, different rhymes.

The millennium is a bit like the British weather,
Always changing,
But as regular as clockwork.

Alisha Kaur Chhatwal (11)
Preston Manor High School

BULLY

The bully,
Prowling around the playground,
Stalking his prey,
With his heavy leather jacket
And his heavy black boots,
His spiky red hair
Makes him stand out amongst the crowd.
Suddenly he stops
And starts heading straight for the new kid,
The bully starts on him
And the new kid answers back
Uh-oh! Deep trouble.

Jake Whinn (13)
Preston Manor High School

BULLIES

Bullies they come to you
Like a ton of bricks.
They think they are bad
But they're not
They are just cowards
They pick on people with no friends and no self esteem.
The victim feels like they are in no-man's-land.
They are scared out of their wits.
They make fun of you
But the bullies are acting like fools.
Bullies will beat you up and take your money
But that is not funny.
Bullies, who needs them
Well I know I don't.

Dhurmesh Vekaria (13)
Preston Manor High School

THE DAY THE LAB BLEW UP!

There once was a boy called David
Who once was doing some science
He took two chemicals but one was the wrong one
He mixed them together, which was bad enough
He put them on a Bunsen burner on a roaring flame
Not a good idea
He put in some salt
Even worse
After about 20 seconds of burning
Boom!
He promptly blew up the lab.

There *once* was a boy called David.

David Wilke (12)
Preston Manor High School

THOSE BULLIES

I don't know what to do,
I don't know what to say!
I am just thinking about that gang
Who stop me every day.

They ask me for money
They ask for my lunch
They tease about my clothes
And say I have got a hunch.

I just hope today,
They don't stop me again
Ask me for money or lunch
Since they have nothing to gain.

I don't know if I should speak up
And tell them it's over.
Or even tell my teachers
How I am treated by those creatures.

Kashmira Gupte (13)
Preston Manor High School

FREEDOM

F ighting to be free
R emembering Canada on the way
E very move is followed by
E nvious slave catchers
D etermined to catch you
O verlooking every move, but at last you
M ake it, free!

Hiren Tailor (12)
Preston Manor High School

LIFE

It's just a four letter word,
But yet it means so much,
From the day you are born to the day you die
Different things cross your path.
Just a long list of experiences,
Life, a mystery to those who live it.

To some it's about feelings,
Love, like and hate
And yet that's all life amounts to,
Time is the essence of change,
Life is just a gamble.

To others it is about knowledge,
Learning to read and write,
Obstacles are always getting in the way,
Tackle them skilfully,
Life is a challenge, face it.

To me life means achievement, good or bad,
The feeling of having some importance,
The chance to have a voice, an opinion
And yet I think to myself,
Life! That's all it is,
Life.

Manisha Ruparellia (13)
Preston Manor High School

GUIDANCE TO A VICTIM

I feel as though I ought to write
To you as a friend
To guide you through right
I know you are being bullied
I see the fear in your eyes
I don't want you to worry
I just want you to read what I write,
Stay calm, sit tight
And don't feel a fright
Stand up to that loser
He's no better than you
But whatever you do
Make sure you tell a teacher
All he wants is attention
To look cool in front of his friends
I personally don't think it's fair
So please *take care!*

Anjali Hathi (13)
Preston Manor High School

BULLIES

I walk down the silent corridor
Happy that everyone's gone home.
Then as a shock,
I'm helplessly pushed against the window ledge
I haven't done anything, I yell.

The screams keep coming
I try to rebel the abuse.
The poisonous fear I have never ends
And even though I wish to die, I keep protecting my body.
The meaningless kicks cause many welts.

I feel senseless,
Petrified
And there's no remedy anyone knows of.
I'm persecuted for being alive
And furious at everyone, including myself.

Then they leave,
Spitting on the floor around my abandoned body.
No one knows,
No one cares,
No one can stop this torture.

Naomei Warner (13)
Preston Manor High School

WHAT CAN WE DO?

Bullies, they come over you
like a sea wave,
over the tiny shells.

Bullies, they come over you
like a ton of bricks over
a weak shelf.

Bullies, they think they rule us
and their little selves.

Bullies, they steal your money
and think they are so funny.

Bullies, they pinch you in your tummy
and make you feel like it's not sunny.

So, what can we do,
not to be flushed down the loo?

Saira Tamuri (13)
Preston Manor High School

VICTIM OF BULLYING

Every day I go to school,
The people are so cruel,
They take my money,
Because they think they are big bunnies.
Every day they take money,
I always tell my mummy.

I hate to go to school,
Even the teachers are cruel,
I can't take it any longer,
The people are much stronger,
When I see a stranger,
I think I'm in danger.

I hate school,
The people think they are so cool,
I try not to act suspicious,
The people are so vicious,
Everywhere I go,
The bullies seem to follow.

Vijay Velji (13)
Preston Manor High School

LOGA

L oga is my name
O f course not everyone calls me that
G oing out I love the best
A nd staying in I hate the most.

Loga Sivasubramaniam (11)
Preston Manor High School

THE BULLY

I was walking there in the darkness,
When a body approached me from behind,
I was thinking about how to react,
Humorous, rude or kind.

He started to chase me,
I was terrified,
Then he attacked me,
I cried and I cried.

He kicked me and he punched me,
I had blood all over me,
The bully didn't even care,
He had put my life in misery.

Krupesh Hirani (13)
Preston Manor High School

JUST YOU WAIT!

I hated her
she was ponderous
she always got
away with murder.

She was pompous,
she was vicious,
but I would
not take it.

I was obnoxious,
I was fuming,
I got her alone
at home time and
she got a year's
worth of beatings.

Nadia Giovetti (13)
Preston Manor High School

GOODBYE BLUE SKY

I walk into the dull playground
he's hovering round
his prey
he hunts like an eagle
I'm the prey today.

I creep into my class
I made it at last
but I know
he'll be back
to thump my back.

It's lunchtime
it's time for me to dine
but this time he won't get a nickel,
not even a single dime.

It's time to leave school
I'll try to act cool
but he's there, the same place
wanting me to feel like a fool.

I suppose I'll say goodbye
As this is the last time I'll see the sky.

Naida Hutchinson (13)
Preston Manor High School

ANOTHER DAY

The alarm clock's gone,
It's another day.
Punches to block,
Money to pay.

Walking to school,
Trying to get on time,
But the bullies will follow me
And terrorise my mind.

Punch me, slap me,
Kick me to the ground.
Throw me in a ditch
So I can't be found.

I've done nothing to the bullies
Nothing at all.
Is it because of my glasses
Or is it because I'm small?

But one day, my mind will blow,
I'll make a stand
And put my foot right where it
Lands!

Lianna Lambert (13)
Preston Manor High School

BULLYING

A bully shows no mercy,
He beats a little boy in nursery,
Obnoxious, oblivious, he needs a remedy,
He's just put three kids into therapy!

He runs around,
He doesn't care,
He's giving out a scary stare.
He's grabbed a kid, he's holding tight,
He's given this boy quite a fright!

Tina Gohil (13)
Preston Manor High School

CHILDREN OF THE DEVIL

Who are bullies?
They are the creation of the devil
You don't want to be one of them
You don't want to be their prey.

They will stalk you
They close in on the prey
When you are alone
They put you in hell.

They give you pain
They make you cry
They give you torment
They give you bruises.

They bully you.

If you don't stand up for yourself
Who is going to break your fall into hell?

They are the children of the devil
They are evil.

Mit Padaliya (13)
Preston Manor High School

VICTIM

I am petrified in the playground,
No one knows what I am feeling.
Not knowing what's going to happen next,
Hoping he's ill or away.

His big body
Casting a shadow down on me.
Looking up far to find his face
Looking down towards me with that terrifying grin
The grin paralyses me while I'm beaten up
Because I forgot my dinner money.

Walking with bruised legs
Down that long lane that seems a hundred miles away
While in my mind running through the beatings they gave me,
Looking down seeing my blood
Thinking I should run away.

Devin Chitroda (13)
Preston Manor High School

BULLYING

There's this girl in my class
I really hate her
She thinks she is all that
But she's not
She's so ponderous.

There's this girl in my class
She gets away with everything
She's so affluent
I had to do something about it
Then I got really angry.

I went over to her,
She was all alone
I was red hot
I pushed her and took her money
She just laid there crying.

Kirsty Seager (13)
Preston Manor High School

THE ECLIPSE

It's August the 10th
And the eclipse will be here soon.
My mum said it was something
To do with the sun and the moon.

I dreamt of a parade,
I dreamt of fighting,
I dreamt about sunlight,
I dreamt of their lightning.

There was one more day to go,
So I put on my best outfit,
My Reebok trousers, my Reebok top,
And my jumper that had a Nike tick.

I was having my usual snack
And then I was off to sleep.
I had the most boring dream,
I dreamt of a huddle of sheep.

I just woke up and the day was here,
I was having so much fun,
Just to see the most boring thing,
The moon cover the sun.

Andrew Caesar (13)
Preston Manor High School

BULLYING IS BAD

B ullying is frightening
U sually obnoxious
L iving life in fear
L eaves me terrified
Y elling and shouting
I ndignity myself
N ight and day
G oing to sleep is a nightmare.

I t's cruel what they do
S ometimes I wonder why

B ullying is frightening
A fter all
D ay by day it gets worse.

Supesh Nanji (13)
Preston Manor High School

A DOLPHIN'S LIFE

Earth!
The blue and green planet
Earth is my home,
This is where I live.
I'm a dolphin, a frail one
may I add.

My friends have died in oil spills.
Now it's my turn to go.
As the careless fishermen cause
my early death.
In the deep blue, green sea.

I'm trapped between a decision.
Life or death but there
is only one person to turn to
who will only understand.

If there is a sea god may he
release me from this nightmare.
Like a clock ticking away just
a few minutes till eternal sleep.
Now I must die.
The friendliest creature beneath
the sea.

Prithpal Bhachu (12)
Preston Manor High School

LATE

'Late for games again, Jenkins,
What's your excuse this time?'
'My brother Sir,'
What about your brother?'
'He threw up, Sir,'
'Where?'
'In the car, Sir.'
'Where is he now?'
'At the doctor's'
'Right, let's do games,'
'Can't, Sir,'
'Why?'
'No kit, Sir,'
'Where is it?'
'In the washing machine, Sir,'
'Why?'
''Cause my brother threw up on it.'

Tobias Akash Shanker (11)
Preston Manor High School

The Bully

A coward they say makes a bully
Someone who knows no better,
Than to torment people smaller than they are.
I do not understand so far.

For I do not fear a teacher
And I know how it feels to be bullied,
For years it was me being victimised,
The evidence was incriminating.

I longed for someone to stand by my side,
Instead they watched me suffer
And chanted whilst the bully struck me with a cosh.

I decided I would take my revenge,
Not to beat the bully,
But to join the bully in his evil ways,
Striking fear in children's eyes.

Vikash Vadher (13)
Preston Manor High School

Thug Victim

It was 7.30, I got to school early,
There were these two bullies sitting by the tree
Staring at me. They walked to me,
They were bullying me, then they kicked me in my knee.
They pulled out a stick and they hit me.

I went to tell a teacher, who wouldn't believe me.
At break I tried to run away but they called me 'a gay'.
I ran away but they caught me up and destroyed me.
I fell to the ground and felt very obnoxious.

At lunch I had enough to get my lunch,
The rest of the money was to get me home.
They came up to me and said 'Have you got some money?'
I said 'No,' but they didn't believe me.
They searched me and found the money that I had
So they called me 'a liar'.

After school I thought that I was free but
They were waiting behind the gates.
They picked me up and threw me to the gates,
Slapped me on the face and called me
'A disgrace to the human race'.

Azizi Foster & Mantas Poderys (13)
Preston Manor High School

THE BULLY

Oblivious I am,
Ponderous he is,
Humiliation I stand for,
Domination is me,
Giving up is a dream,

No hesitation, no optimism,
My goals I have to achieve,
Meaningless feelings,
Senseless thoughts,
That doesn't bother me,
'Cause I'm in charge of the world.

Harder, harder I try to be,
Colder than reptiles I am,
I know what I am,
And know what I want,
Depressing and oppressing is my job.

Judith Idakula (13)
Preston Manor High School

BULLYING

I hate going to school,
I think bullies rule,
Every day I get bullied,
I can't stand it,
It gets me worried.

I can't take it for any longer,
Every day they get stronger and stronger,
If it carries on I'll lose my temper,
If I tried to tell the teacher,
I think I would regret it for ever and ever.

There is nothing I can do or say,
For if it weren't for bullies,
I wouldn't be this way.

Neeten Patel & Dipak Chauhan (13)
Preston Manor High School

THINGS I LOVE AND THINGS I HATE

PlayStation, my favourite computer games
Big, brave, soldiers with swords and shields,
Red motorbikes, shiny silver metal, brakes and horn: *'Parp!'*
I like those games!

Pink, white and very sweet
Cold - it makes my tongue shiver
Strawberry ice-cream -
I like that stuff!

White and long like worms
Yukky, horrible
Spaghetti -
I hate that stuff!

I'm scared of heights
I fall off, hurt myself
Climbing frames -
I hate those things!

Navatheesan Navakumar (12)
Preston Manor High School

MY SOCKS

I've had these socks
that are covered in dots
for ages and ages and ages.

They looked okay
before the affray
that changed the colour
to bright pink and white.
Oohh . . . what a sight, and they stayed that way
for ages and ages and ages.

The heels fell off
when in the wash.
You can see my ankles
they go black now like soot and stay that way
for ages and ages and ages.

I hate the smell
well . . .
that make it, it's time for them to go
for ages and ages and ages.

Nia Barnabie (12)
Preston Manor High School

I'M A BULLY

I like to wander through the playground,
Arrogant and obnoxious.
Everyone stares up at me petrified and scared,
As I start violent and vicious fights.

I like to touch other pupils' belongings,
When they all go confidently off to PE.
Cunningly and slyly I open up their wallets and bags,
Loving to hear them say innocently,
'Who took my dinner money?'

I like to pick on small, dwarf kids,
Who wouldn't stand a chance of liberating themselves.
I like to pick on dumbstruck nerds,
Who wouldn't speak a word for themselves.

I like to bully others,
Because it's the only way of getting rid of my tyrant anger,
And is the only way
Of escaping the grief of my parents' separation.

So when tomorrow comes,
Everyone will be on a lookout for me.
But they all will know that for me,
Tomorrow will just be another day.

Rakesh Pattni (13)
Preston Manor High School

THINGS I LIKE AND HATE

I come home
My mum has to make it
My dad has to bake it
But I have to eat it
Pizza!
I like it

I get it from school
With the attitude
My mum says to do it
But I hate it
Homework!
I hate it a lot.

Jasmeet Panesar (12)
Preston Manor High School

BULLIES

Bullies think they are cool,
They think they are in control,
But actually they are cowards.
They think they are powerful and stronger,
Mostly they are older.
Looking around seeing people getting bullied
Looks bad.
So what can be done?
Bullies are tall and normally big built.
The victims mostly appear as weaklings.
Bullies move around in groups of 4 or 5,
Bossing everyone around.
Calling everyone names,
Hitting them etc.
Bullies are attention-seeking.
They may be lacking care and love at home.
If you are a victim,
Do something.
Stand up for yourself,
Fight the bullies
To end their nasty habit.

Aarti Patel (12)
Preston Manor High School

DRIVE YOUR TEACHER NUTS

'Why were you absent yesterday, young man?'
'I got my teeth pulled out, Sir.'
'Really, let's see?'
'I can't open my mouth, Sir.
'How are you talking then?'

'*Mmmmm* (I'm not, Sir)'
'Pardon? Speak with your mouth, young man.'
'I can't, Sir'
'You just did!'
'Did not, Sir!'

'Where's your uniform?'
'It's in the wash, Sir.'
'Why didn't you wash it?'
'I can't wash it.'
'Why not?'

'I'm allergic to the powder, Sir.'
'Forget it, go and do PE!'
'Can't, Sir.'
'Why?'
'I haven't got my PE kit.'

'Why not?'
'It's in the wash, Sir.'
'Who usually washes it?'
'Dad, Sir.'
'Where's your dad?'
'Dead, Sir.'

'That's the fifth this week.'
'I know, Sir.
My mum marries a lot.'
'Go, I don't wanna see you
For the rest of the day.'

Shalini Parjan (11)
Preston Manor High School

THE BIG BAD BULLY

I'm the bully,
The big, bad bully,
I beat them with my rod,
The poor little sod.

I huff and puff furiously,
As they walk away curiously,
Little did they know that I'm the bully,
I show contempt for everyone.

I'm meaningless in my palace,
The queen calls me a fool,
But at school I rule,
As I am so cruel.

I remain unremorseful,
Yet I feel abandoned.
But I'm the bully,
The big, bad bully.

The queen has made me what I am,
A terrorist in the kingdom,
Persecuted in her land.
Who will solve the puzzle
And turn me into a lamb?

Anika Kaul (13)
Preston Manor High School

IS IT RIGHT TO DO SO?

Everyone can be a victim.
Suffering is what I cause.
I do it at home.
I am not encouraged to do so
But I do it anyway.

Everyone can be a victim
In his/her own way.
I intimidate at school.
Am I encouraged to do so?
Yes!

Everyone can be a victim.
Victims sometimes victimise.
I am not a bully at work.
Regardless of encouragement
I remember the hurt I caused.

Neer Mehta (13)
Preston Manor High School

THE BEE

There once was a lonely bee,
Who sat in a lonely tree.
He had left his hive,
Because he wanted to survive,
But all the madness in his house,
He thought he'd be better as a mouse.
The bee finally died on a branch.
And fell down like an avalanche.

Sunit Patel (11)
Preston Manor High School

EVERYONE

It all starts at home,
I was being affronted,
Suffering from indignity,
I was petrified!

It then started at school,
The pupils first,
Then the teachers,
Everyone was being vicious,
I was petrified!

Will it start at work?
Will the boss be obnoxious?
Will he treat with senseless actions?
Will everyone be offensive?
Will I be petrified?

Hiten Khatri (13)
Preston Manor High School

UP IN SPACE

I'd like to see the stars,
Go flying around Venus and Mars,
If I could land on the moon,
My next stop would be Neptune,
I believe that there are Martians out there,
When they see earthlings all they'll do is stare, stare, stare,
I wouldn't dare go near the sun, I'd get burnt alive,
I'd much prefer going to Saturn,
I can't decide where to go,
As there are so many places to explore
Up in space!

Sapna Shah (11)
Preston Manor High School

The Bully

I am the bully
I will always be
The obnoxious things I do
I love to pick on my victims
Just you wait and see

All I want is money
To be affluent
Affronting their mothers
I punch them into a daze
Just you wait and see

I glimpse down at them viciously
I treat them like dirt
The ponderous things
I will never give up
Just you wait and see.

Shilpa Mepani (14) & Jayne Lake (13)
Preston Manor High School

Thugs

I was overjoyed when I harassed and tortured the kid,
I was suspended.
I did not go to school that week,
oh what fun I had,
playing computer games on my own.

But I did not enjoy it for long,
it got boring.
Just watching TV on my own,
the little weasel who told of me,
watching Power Rangers cheered me up.

I had to go back to school,
oh the homework I had to catch up with.
I attacked the rascal again,
I got suspended,
oh yes, another week off school.

Gaurang Pattni (13) & Trinesh Champaneri (14)
Preston Manor High School

MY LIFE!

When I was one
I sucked my thumb.
When I was two
I started to wear shoes
When I was three
I got stung by a bee
When I was four
I toppled onto the floor
When I was five
I cut myself with a knife
When I was six
I loved eating pick 'n' mix
When I was seven
I went to Devon
When I was eight
I visited the Tate
When I was nine
I was looking fine
When I was ten
I broke up with my friend
Now I'm eleven
But I wish I was seven!

Amira Nassr & Saima Jaffar (11)
Preston Manor High School

MY HATES AND DISLIKES

Graciousness and happiness,
People contain that inside but don't use it
I hate that stuff.

Family and friends
Combine their love
I like that stuff.

Football and tennis
Both great sports
I like that stuff.

People dying
Lack of food
I hate that stuff.

People playing at playtime
Having fun
I like that stuff.

Selfish people
Take it for themselves
I hate that stuff.

Love and friendship
Happily together
I love that stuff.

Jason Craig (11)
Preston Manor High School

THUG

I see the vicious bully
The obnoxious, furious,
Offensive bully, with no remorse, standing in front of me.
My heart racing every day,
I hesitantly stand with apprehension.

I shiver and tremble in fear,
The wrathful, intimidating bully.
He comes towards me sometimes,
Even beckons me.
He approaches me, I shiver with sheer fear.

Playtime's over, I fell with decorous excitement,
But then he threatens me
Saying he'd be back.
I go inside the obstreperous school building
Not looking forward to the next break time
I wish I would be liberated from my miserable dreary life.

Kashmeer Savani (13)
Preston Manor High School

MY MUM

I love my mum,
She gives money,
So I go and get some sweets.
I also get some school lunch.
My mum's a good cook,
She's very kind to me,
She makes the best food,
That's why she's a great mum to me!

Sagar Pandya (11)
Preston Manor High School

I Hate...

I hate,
all the things on my plate,
like peas,
and cheese,
and tea as long as it's sweet,
and then broccoli.

I hate,
Andy Cole,
scoring goals,
German is devastating
I also hate reading.

I hate,
music,
and the school footie kit,
I hate English,
and Religion,
I hate cricket,
and the noise 'Ribbit.'

I hate . . .

Curtis Layne (11)
Preston Manor High School

Myself

T   erri is my name
E   ating is my fame
R   aspberries are my favourite fruit
R   ound and small children are cute
I   live life to the full.

Terri Bull (11)
Preston Manor High School

I LIKE/HATE THAT THING

I like to play on it
My dad likes to work on it,
Our computer,
I like that thing.

My mum likes to make it
I like to eat it,
Pizza,
I like that thing.

I'll always be with it
My parents love it,
Brothers,
I hate that thing.

Teachers love to give me it
I hate to do it,
Homework,
I hate that thing.

Sneha Patel (11)
Preston Manor High School

SOMETIMES

Sometimes I feel as fit as a tiger,
Sometimes I feel as happy as a lottery winner.
Sometimes I feel as sad as a turtle.
Sometimes I feel as lonely as a worm.
Sometimes I feel as dumb as a lunatic,
Sometimes I feel as pretty as a princess.
Sometimes I feel as clever as a scientist,
But however I feel, I'm always me.

Linda Vlasaku (11)
Preston Manor High School

MY HATES AND LIKES

Cricket, the game I like.
Batting the ball I like.
Cricket.
I like that stuff . . .

Nice and yummy.
Tasty and bubbly.
Pizza.
I like that stuff . . .

Slimy like snails.
Yukky like anything.
Apple pie.
I hate that stuff . . .

Hard as stone.
Bitter like aloes.
Sprouts.
I hate that stuff . . .

Fiazau Khalid (11)
Preston Manor High School

MY FAVOURITE T-SHIRT

I have had this T-shirt since I was young
But now it's a piece of junk
and has been so for days and days and days.

It was supposed to be multicoloured
but I used it as my teddy
cos I carried it everywhere
and did so for days and days and days.

The arms ripped off
in the wash
and you can see my chest
exposed by my vest
and has been so for days and days and days.

As my favourite T-shirt goes
I'll give it to my Aunt Mog to sew
and once again I'll look neat
on the street
and will remain for days and days and days.

Sajeevithan Puvaneswaran (12)
Preston Manor High School

THE PLAYGROUND

The playground is full of sound,
These can be very easily found.
The tapping of the tins,
The bashing of bins
Makes the playground its own orchestra.

It's time to run out,
The children love to be out and about.
The bullies are here,
The shy ones fear,
Don't worry, it'll soon be time to disappear.

The music is flowing,
The children are going,
Balls are bouncing
Like tigers who are pouncing.

Nikita Kotecha (11)
Preston Manor High School

HOMEWORK EXCUSES

'No homework again Kavish?
What is the excuse this time?'
'Not my fault, Sir.'
'Who's fault is it then?
My mum's, Sir.'
'Mum? What did she do?'
'She got sick, Sir.'
'But, what has that got to do with your homework?'
'She couldn't help me, Sir.'
'That's the third time this term.'
'I know Sir, it is very upsetting, Sir.'
'How is your mum then?'
'She's fine.'
'I thought you said she was ill.'
'Yeah, but that was yesterday, Sir.'
'Well then, where is your homework?'
'At home Sir.'
'Why is it at home then?'
'My mum's finishing it.'
'But your mum is supposed to be helping you,
not doing it for you.'
'I know Sir, I told her what the homework is about,
she's doing the rest.'
'But that is not how it works!'
'Well, it works for me, Sir.'

Kavish Abbas (11)
Preston Manor High School

PLEASE MRS BUTLER

'Please Mrs Butler!
This boy, Derek Drew keeps copying my work
Miss, what shall I do?'

'Go on the roof, my dear
Go and sit in the sink
Do whatever you think.'

'Please Mrs Butler !
This girl Marie Drew keeps taking my rubber
Miss, what shall I do?'

'Hold it in your hand
Hold it in your vest
Do whatever you think best.'

'Please Mrs Butler this girl Shelley
This girl Shelley Owen keeps poking me with a
Pencil. Miss, what shall I do?'

'Poke her back
Go and sit away from her.
Do whatever you think.'

'Please Mrs Butler!
This boy Michael Owen
Keeps hiding my lunch, Miss, what shall I do?'

Hide his lunch
Go home and eat.
Do whatever you think best
But don't ask me, my dear!'

Maryam Ijaz (11)
Preston Manor High School

MATILDA!

Her name is Matilda
She is 6 years old
She loves to read books
She loves to read
She loves computers so much,
that her brother started to call her Computer Nerd.

She hates her parents,
her parents hate her.
Her parents are very posh
and her brother's name is Josh.

She would love to go to school
Her dad said suddenly 'You are going to school.'
She was very happy.

Suddenly she found that she's got magic!

She saw her head teacher
her head teacher hated her
and guess what?
Matilda hated her too.

She came home crying
she wanted her teacher
to be her mother.
So she moved to her teacher's house
and decided to never see her parents again.

Fozia Rahman (11)
Preston Manor High School

EXCUSES, EXCUSES

'English homework out on the table!
Where's yours Kiran?'
'Not on the table, Sir.'
'Where is it then?'
'Ashley's got it.'
'Why's he got it?'
'He wants to copy it.'
'Where's last week's homework?'
'Andrew's got it.'
'Why on Earth has he got it?'
'He said that he'll put it on display.'
'Where's he now?'
'Gone.'
'Gone where?'
'Fishing.'
'Where?'
'In the middle of the Atlantic Ocean.'
'Will he be all right?'
'Nah!'
'When are you going to get it back?'
'When he gets back.'
'When?'
'Dunno.'
'What?'
'Never.'
'Never! What do you mean?'
'He's changed schools!'
'Why?'
'Dunno!'

Vasita Patel (11)
Preston Manor High School

THE STREETS AT NIGHT

1.25 am,
I'm walking home on my own.
It's pitch black,
But the neon lights lead the way.
Dusty and musty smells fill the air.
Car fumes, tobacco and whisky I can smell too.
Little cars drive past.
My footsteps are slow and steady.
In my pocket I have a newspaper.
The newspaper says.
'A boy was killed while walking home.
Stabbed in the heart so many times.'
I'm moving a little faster.
Crash!
I jump.
And graze my elbow on the red brick wall,
As a dustbin falls to the ground.
My heart is pounding.
Is someone out there?
Is it my turn to go?
'Miaow!'
Oh it's just a measly cat.
1.45 am.
I'm still walking home on my own.

Dolapo Osonowo (11)
Preston Manor High School

TORNADO'S STRIKE

I cause havoc and destruction
I am fierce and life
I can pierce
I can hurl up houses and no less.
People hide
I can collide.

Houses and buildings destroyed
Towns wrecked
Finally things nearly get back to
the way they were
Waiting for it to strike again.

It strikes again
The people have been through hell and beyond.

Bhavin Patel (11)
Preston Manor High School

THE LONG AWAITED DAY!

There are just over two months to the *millennium* -
it's just round the corner and it's great!
We'd better start preparations before it's too late!

As the clock hand strikes midnight,
everyone will be waiting,
The wonderful atmosphere shining bright.

I cannot wait for the long awaited moment;
and the day to come, so hurry!
Until then it's just me counting the days -1, 2, 3!

It's here!

Afshan Khan (12)
Preston Manor High School

EXCUSES, EXCUSES!'

'Late again, Prithpal,
What's the excuse this time?'
'Not my fault, Sir.'
'Whose fault is it then?'
'Dad's, Sir.'
'Your dad, what did he do?'
'We had a father and son fight
And I killed him.'
'You had a father and son fight last week and you killed him.
And you're always late on history days.'
'But that's the only day, it's a religious thing.'
'So you have more than one dad?'
'No, Sir.'
'Then where are your dads?'
'Dead, Sir. It's very upsetting.'

Dhimal Varsani (11)
Preston Manor High School

BULLY

He says he's had enough
But he hasn't seen the rest,
He says I am not obnoxious,
Well, he should watch his back,
He is going to get it.

He tried to retaliate by putting some superglue on my chair
But I was too clever for him,
Today at lunchtime I started to retaliate,
I tripped him over,
And I asked him, 'How dangerous can you get?'
Now he is falling behind in class because he never comes to class.

But I have to give in to him
He complained to the council,
I am going to be prosecuted,
I am in big trouble,
It started with a joke, now it is serious.

Mohammed Al-Tarehi (13)
Preston Manor High School

GREEN

Green is the grass,
And the leaves of the trees,
Green is the smell,
Of a country breeze.

Green is a shelter,
Where the moss is made,
Green is hiding,
In the shade.

Green is a flutter,
That comes in spring,
Green is mixed
With everything.

Green is the end
Where I cannot live,
Green is my life,
That I cannot give.

Green is mixed with honeysuckle vine,
Green is yours,
Green is mine.

Krishni Kunasingham (12)
Preston Manor High School

THE FEROCIOUS

As clumsy me arrived at class
I stared out the window glass
I heard the famous verse repeat
'Mary, Mary don't dirty my seat.'

It's break
and guess what, I'm the fisher's bait.
First a kick then a punch
Then they took all my lunch.

My parents think I take away their dignity
Because of my stupidity
They are oblivious
they treat us like aliens.

They torture me fully,
the ferocious bullies
They never let me leave their sight
They haunt me throughout the night.

It takes away my dignity, my pride
How will I ever survive?

Chrizelle Strydom & Pooja Shah (13)
Preston Manor High School

THE SHOP

Dogs barking mad,
Rats being ever so bad.

Cats chasing their tails,
Hamsters holding onto the rails.

Parrots squawking,
Customers talking.

Little children jumping up and down,
Mummy's got a big frown.

Time to close,
People go.

Nothing left,
Not even theft.

Faiza Khalid (11)
Preston Manor High School

PUSHING US AWAY!

They affront anyone who comes their way,
because compared to them we are nothing,
like wild animals liberated, it's outrageous.
I don't know why we tolerate it,
They push and shove.
making sure we worship one god, and one god only, them!

When we tell the teachers all they can say is -
'That's nice love,' pushing us away
as if they couldn't care less what happens.
The bullies just stare and laugh,
How humiliating for us victims.

Sometimes I feel as if I am an alien from outer space -
and that I don't belong here in their territory.
I feel as if I'm a turtle in a shell too scared to come out,
but it's like there's no way to escape,
it's like a bad nightmare which won't go away.

Nisha Kent (13)
Preston Manor High School

WHEN I FELL IN LOVE WITH YOU

W hen I fell in love with you
H andsome and sensitive person
E verything about you is so good
N othing else but you is true.

I 'm head over heels.

F ell in love with you and only you.
E verything I care about
L ooks just like you
L oving you every day.

I n my heart I would never forget you
N owadays I'm lonely too.

L etting everyone know how I feel.
O ver you and only you.
V ery nice to me at times
E very day I think about you.

W ith all my heart
I love you
T alking about you every day my
H eartbeat races every time I see you.

Y ou are my life
O h you are so fine
U fill my heart with joy and love.

Tola Lawal (11)
Preston Manor High School

THUG

First he shouted at me,
For no reason at all,
Then he made me sit in the corner
And confiscated my ball.

He made me really furious,
I couldn't take this anymore,
I got up and cursed him,
So he whipped my back sore.

He was really obnoxious,
This is really outrageous,
So I got up and left the school.
I felt really courageous.

Ramesh Gorasia (14) & Jai Patel (13)
Preston Manor High School

SCHOOL HORROR

8.45 the school bell rings,
Now I fear as the horror begins,
Snigger, sneer, rude remarks,
That is all how it starts.

Bawl, bellow, belt, and call.
They're not interested at all.
Broken nose, no backbone,
All because of a stone.

3.20 the school will end.
Over the weekend I will mend.
Safe and sound I shall be
Until Monday comes to be.

Neetisha Lakhani (14) & Anita Marwaha (13)
Preston Manor High School

THE VICTIM

There is a boy in my class
offensive, perplexing, arrogant.
Rude and abusive as can be
bullying everyone including me.
Determined to be top of the *heap.*

Yesterday Mr Vicious hit out at authority
ferocious, meaningless and persistent.
That cost him the school's equivalent
of a prison sentence.

The next day he was back ready to rebel
he was oblivious and obnoxious.
What a scandal!
He was outraged with an obsession
to hurt anyone who came in his way.

Deepika Vaja & Hetal Taeler (13)
Preston Manor High School

THE THUG'S VICTIM

It happened when I was in school,
the headmaster, I knew, was very cruel.
He influenced my mind with hate,
when I left school it was too late.

He never accepted me,
for what I was to be.
The way he acted was suspicious,
he was also very vicious.

I told my teacher but he did not care,
the way he acted was not very fair.
My classmates did not understand,
so they did not help me or give me a hand.

I was all alone and isolated,
this made me feel exasperated.
When I was in school I was not tolerated,
but now I shall be liberated.

Jagree Wathanasilapa & Fazila Mohamed (13)
Preston Manor High School

THE BULLY

School began,
He felt bad.
There he went
Into the school gates.

There he was
Standing by.
He couldn't move
His little leg.

There he was
Beaten, pushed and insulted.
While his friends
Were just watching.

When it was over
He felt stupid for
doing that thing
which he would not
tell a soul.

Meha Patel (13)
Preston Manor High School

A BAD DAY

I went into school on Monday morning,
And walked into the gates,
I saw the bully standing there and yawning,
Then he ran up to me and punched me in the face!

That same day I went into the hall,
To go and eat my lunch,
He put his foot out and made me fall,
And I heard my arm go crunch!

I felt the pain, I felt the shame,
Going through my head,
Just instead of breathing now
I wish that I was *dead!*

Louise Harman (13)
Preston Manor High School

BULLY

Harry, ponderous and brainy,
Affluent but fragile,
Loaded with money,
My ideal prey.

Harry, ponderous and brainy,
Teacher's treasure,
Mummy's baby, Daddy's doll,
My ideal prey.

Harry, ponderous and brainy,
Lonely and terrified,
Goody goody
Meaningless, brainy
My ideal prey.

Dhiren Tailor (14)
Preston Manor High School

THE BULLY

Lurking around the playground,
Like a hungry wolf,
Looking for a helpless boy,
To eat and engulf.

I see one in my sights,
I can smell his scent,
His clothes all washed and clean,
His money was well spent.

I creep up behind him,
Push him on the ground,
He is too scared,
He can't make a sound.

I crouch down next to him,
Ask him for his money,
He gives me 50p,
So I punched him in the tummy.

I cannot believe it,
Is that all he gives,
I've got to have some more,
Cos' the big bully lives!

Rohit Gami (13)
Preston Manor High School

THE VICTIM

Now and then every day,
I'm sad and feel ungrateful,
Everyone laughing,
I am feeling indignity from everyone around me.

Exasperated is not the word,
It's worse than that.
Beats from left, right and centre,
My parents say it's obnoxious,
But they do the same.

I don't have anyone to turn to,
I can't see a shoulder to cry on,
I'm a loner and there's nothing to it.
Everyone hates me, beats me up,
Just because I have the brains, and they don't.
It's jealousy.

Sharika Varshani (13)
Preston Manor High School

BULLYING

School began at 8.45am,
The boys at school started on me,
They were saying nasty remarks,
The boy was rich,
They said that my face was clumsy.

One boy came and said, 'Stop this.'
They are refusing to give up,
The three boys started even more,
I told them I'd tell the teacher.

The teacher came out,
She shouted,
'Tommy and Johnny
I am furious with you,
Get back to class.'

Kunil Nana (13)
Preston Manor High School

BULLYING

She is a nerd.
She has an obnoxious body.
She is abusive.
She is awkward and outrageous.

She talks about everyone,
And is a spoilt brat.
She is oblivious about us,
As I pushed her against the wall.

She loves to do her homework,
As she is all goody, goody.
She dresses like a nerd,
And is so ferocious.

She is remorseless,
As well as senseless and meaningless.
She nearly killed the girl,
As she was bleeding.

Help her, help her,
She's really gone mad.
She has problems in her life
Which caused all this.

Deepti Nandha (13)
Preston Manor High School

DREAMS AND WISHES

Looking through the window,
Thinking about what to do,
Thinking about my life,
And what I have been through.

Been through love,
Been through hate,
Been through day
And been through night.

Wishing one day
All dreams would come true,
And hoping that my wishes would come true,
And what the future holds for me will be good.

Reena Parmar (13)
Preston Manor High School

FASHION!

Clothes and shoes, bags and coats,
Are everything,
That is everything.

In my world there's names for clothes,
Just like people they comfort me,
I love fashion,
It's my world.

Fashion is here,
Fashion is there,
When you look it's everywhere,
I'll tell you when you see me,
You will know what I am on about.

Purvi Patel (13)
Preston Manor High School

THE SEAGULL

She spread her white wings
and got ready to fly,
and took off into the light blue ocean sky.
She flew further and further
into the mist,
hoping she hadn't been missed.
As her snow-white wings spread through the sky,
she wondered why the sky had turned pale green.
matching the colour of her eyes?
She slowly flew down to her nest and fell asleep.

Jeshma Raithatha (12)
Rooks Heath High School

MAGPIE

A cunning crook, a crafty spy,
Who knows what will catch his eye.
A bottle top or a diamond ring,
Or some other shiny thing.
Glossy waistcoat, raven head,
One, unlucky it is said.
A villain with a beady eye,
A robber that has wings to fly.
The burglar bird of daylight theft,
I wonder where its loot is kept.

Jessie Wear (12)
Rooks Heath High School

FUTURE OF THE WORLD

I have a dream for the future that
All countries will be equal
In money and wealth.
We have to save them from poverty,
Not give them silly old dime.

I have a dream for the future that
We will be able to see all countries happy,
Having the same fun as other countries.
God created the world so that all
Countries will be equal and loving.

I have a dream for the future that
There will be no one bullying you
Because your country is poor or unpopular.
Still countries have to work their way out of poverty.
Most countries want to be on the top of the world.
All countries will be happy with what God gave them.

Zahra Latifi (13)
Rooks Heath High School

THIEF STEALING . . .

I saw a thief
Steal my TV
And take it to his flat.
He stole the cups,
He stole the plates,
He stole the welcome mat.

He stole the bed,
He stole the chair,
He stole the cat,
And the desk,
And the refrigerator.

He went out to a cafe,
I used a bunch of skeleton keys
And stole into his place.
When the thief got back home
And found me in the bed
He was annoyed and turned
A criminal shade of red.

I said do not worry,
I sleep as quiet as a mouse,
And anyway hadn't he
Just moved me to this house?

Anjli Vakani (13)
Rooks Heath High School

POLLUTION

Oil on beaches, car exhausts and litter,
Affects our world,
So stop throwing litter and start recycling,
The world will be a cleaner place.
Pollution affects animals, birds and
The human race.
So less cars, more bikes,
More bins, less litter,
Less factories, more cleaner air.
So stop littering and start
Recycling!

Louise Hartley (12)
Rooks Heath High School

UTOPIA - MY PERFECT WORLD

Peace would be everywhere.
Everyone would live in harmony together.
Racism would be ruled out;
For this is utopia.
Everyone would have a say in how they were treated.
Children would be paid to go to school.
There will be safety everywhere.
Indecent behaviour would not be accepted.
Offensive people would be treated accordingly.
No one would ever be able to live in a world like this.

Amy Edwards (12)
Rooks Heath High School

UTOPIA

In my perfect world there would be no violence or confrontation
And nothing would go wrong, everything would be fine,
Everyone would have their fair share of things,
If people had something to say they would say it with no fear!
No one would judge anyone,
We wouldn't have to go to school,
We would have equal amounts of money,
We wouldn't have to get out of bed until we wanted to!
There would be no illness or disease!
This would be my perfect world!

Prudence Silk (12)
Rooks Heath High School

VOLCANO

She bubbled with anger,
As the people crowded the tiny island
She covered the crops with rock; she chased them with hunger.

She stirred up trouble,
Thinking they'll go away,
She put her strength together by double.

She threw a tantrum,
Then she hit the island by surprise,
She ruined the little island then she realised she was being dumb.

The little island was history
Because of her selfishness.
Now this island may never have its glory.

Dayani Balasubramaniyem (11)
Roxeth Manor Middle School

CHICKEN AND WINE

Chicken, chicken, is so fine!
It is better than my wine.
Chicken is white
And wine is red,
When it's drunk - it goes to my head.
Chicken is meat
And wine is drink,
I can do without wine,
But I must eat.
Chicken for lunch and dinner and tea,
It's the only thing that can satisfy me!

Gemma Keady
St Anne's RC High School For Girls

THE TIGER

The tiger will strike at night,
The tiger will strike with might,
The tiger will strike today,
The tiger will make you pay,

It will make you pay, for what you did,
You threw away the key and shut the lid,
You put the tiger in a cell,
For others to see and to tell,

For what? For money? Yes of course,
You took the tiger from its course,
You took from the tiger, being wild,
Your punishment will not be so mild.

Morgan Hallé
St Anne's RC High School For Girls

MY UNCOOL FAMILY

My family is so uncool,
Don't mention parents' night at school,
My mum goes mad,
And blames it on my dad.

Then there's my brother,
He's just like my mother.
He's so annoying and takes the mick,
My sister thinks she's a groovy chick.

I'm the one who is really cool,
I'm the most normal one of all.

Jeanette Martel (12)
St Anne's RC High School For Girls

SCHOOL FRIENDS

I look around the school building,
All I see is different faces.
Some are friendly and happy,
Others are sad and unhappy.
Then in the corner of the hallway
There's a group of girls,
They look at me and burst out laughing,
What's wrong with me?
They point and stare,
They make me feel uncomfortable.
I turn around to walk away,
There's a group of other girls behind,
But they don't laugh, they don't point,
They just simply say,
'Would you like to be our friend?'
I answer in surprise,
'Of course I'll be your friend.'
I walk in the middle of two girls,
And as we walk on
I turn around,
The group of girls in the corner
Have stopped laughing and pointing.
I give them a smile,
They give me a dirty look,
But I don't care because I have a group of friends
Who are really nice,
And that's what matters to me.

Caroline Noone
St Anne's RC High School For Girls

A WEIRD CHUM

I have a very special friend,
Who thinks that a friend is a fiend.
She eats her sandwiches crispy,
And wears clothes that are punchy.
She ties her hair up so high,
It makes her face look like a pie.

Her nose never stops dripping,
She never stops creeping.
She acts weird as a wizard,
She even licks her pet lizard.
When she's angry, she's a grizzly bear,
But when she's happy, she's as sweet as a deer.

She never fancies a guy,
And her room is a pig sty.
Her name is Roberta,
She is a great flirter.
She's related to Grant Mitchell,
She comes from hell,
She is a little devil.

Keerthiga Yohananthan (12)
St Anne's RC High School For Girls

CHOCOLATE FEVER!

I get a funny feeling in my tummy,
After I've eaten something yummy,
I'm quite thin,
In fact I'm slim,
But I cannot resist anything scrummy.

It's nice and thick just like a brick,
My favourite bar is the Galaxy stick,
But I've had one too many, it's coming back up,
Splat, I've just been sick.

Alicia Francois-George (12)
St Anne's RC High School For Girls

MY JOURNEY TO SCHOOL

I come down the stairs with my bag on my back,
While my brother is watching TV,
I've had my breakfast, I've made my lunch,
So now I am ready to leave.

I get to the bus stop at the Great Cambridge Road
Where I wait for the bus to come,
At a quarter to eight or a little earlier,
I wait for the 231.

Two buses have gone and one has just come,
But it was full so I'm in a state,
There's one more alternative, the 217,
Now I think I'm going to be late!

Shall I turn back or shall I not?
The time is now 8.11,
It's a bit of a pain, but hold on a minute,
I'm saved, it's the 617!

I'm really worn out, I've arrived at school,
And the time is now a quarter to nine,
I'm in the classroom, and everything is ready,
Thank God I was just on time!

Elisa Jeffery (12)
St Anne's RC High School For Girls

LIFE

Life is wonderful,
just as can be.
Life is precious,
just like gold.
Life is free,
just like a bird.
Life has a meaning,
just like me.
Life is a mystery,
just like magic.
Life is tough,
just like the sea.
Life is like a rubber ball,
just bouncing up and down.
Life is quiet,
just like a mouse.
Life is like a book,
just turning a page.
Life is moving,
just like time.

Sara Catherine Perera Sordillo
St Anne's RC High School For Girls

A TEENAGER!

In one more day I'll be thirteen,
A teenage girl,
A party queen.

No more going to bed at eight,
Teenagers stay up quite late.

Lipsticks, mascara are the trend,
Perfumes are a girl's best friend,
Drive my mother around the bend,
On the phone for hours on end.

Lock away my cuddly toys,
From now on, I'm chasing boys!

Christina Backham
St Anne's RC High School For Girls

WHAT IS GOLD?

When I open my eyes at night,
Gold is the colour I see so bright.
Gold is the richness of every item,
Gold is the paint of a gem outlightened.

Gold is the moonlight shining with the stars,
Gold is the symbol of people's richness,
And their cars.
Gold is expensive when buying a wedding ring,
Gold is thinking of a dream,
That isn't just another thing.

Gold is the church bell going ding, dong,
Gold is in Tina Turner's 'Golden Eye' song.
Gold is the richness of the taste in a cherry,
Gold is a scent of expensive jewellery.
Gold is the touch of a newborn baby,
Gold is me as a lovely young lady.

Charlene Boyaram (13)
St Anne's RC High School For Girls

COME AND JOIN ME

Come and join me in the jungle,
    With all the trees and naughty monkeys.

Come and join me in the sky,
    We'll fly over mountains so very high.

Come and join me at the fair,
    We'll go on a roller-coaster if you dare.

Let's go on the spooky rides,
    Then plunge down the gungy slides.

Come and join me by the sun,
    We'll sit on the beach all day long.

Come and join me to see the Queen,
    Make sure your gungy clothes are clean.

Come and join me at home once more,
    We'll watch TV and eat popcorn.

Phoebe Raphael (12)
St Anne's RC High School For Girls

THE OWL

If I were an owl
Flying high in the sky,
What would I see
With my searching eye?
I'd see fields of corn
And barley and wheat
And watch for movement
For something to eat.

A mouse or a vole or a shrew on the ground
Would give me a treat
Keeping my body sound.
I'd glide on the wind
And soar on the breeze
And think, I love my life of ease.

Elizabeth Ainger (12)
St Anne's RC High School For Girls

WHAT DO THE LETTERS OF MY NAME STAND FOR?

M   stands for masterly, making mischief absolutely everywhere I go.
E   stands for elegantly elevating my education and contributing
    knowledge and everything I know.
L   stands for loving life to the full and definitely making the most of it.
I   stands for incredibly indicating my intelligence and positively
    showing every bit of it.
S   stands for sensibly setting standards and conquering every goal
    I make.
S   stands for staying satisfactory, soulful and safe and then hopefully
    I won't meet my fate.
A   is for automatically being aware and making sure I have no doubts.

Unfortunately I don't have another letter that joins my first name,
So that will have to do for now!

Melissa Berry
St Anne's RC High School For Girls

MONEY IS MADE OF LOVE

What is money?
We live for money, we die for money,
Know matter how much we have we all need money.
What is money?
We steal it, we give it, we pay our bills with it,
But can we do without? *No!* we can't do without money,
In the same way we can't do without love,
Because . . .
Where there is love, there is success and where there
Is success there is wealth.
Do you want wealth? Do you want success?
Do you have love? Love is happiness, *God is love.*

Ellen Oparaocha
St Anne's RC High School For Girls

ALONE

O' my dear we're so well matched,
It's just a shame that you're attached,
For if you weren't,
I could show you that I care,
I could show you that I love you,
But until the day you become free to love,
I stand alone,
A lonely friend,
With no one to love and cherish,
And no one to hold through the long lonely nights.

Paul Nichols (15)
St Paul's Catholic College

UNHEARD VOICES

Let's take a seat and listen to,
The words you've got to feed,
Just all you say, all you do,
Is supposed to be what we need.

I think you don't really have a clue,
I bet you really don't.
You say you wanna talk to us
But the more you feed we won't,

Listen to a word you say,
Especially if you shout.
So go on, just carry on,
If you want me to walk out.

You think you know what we are,
And all our hopes and dreams,
But take a second out of your secluded world
And make an effort to know what we mean.

We're supposed to be your life and love.
Yeah! Just make it world-wide known,
You claim to brag about us all the time,
But all we see is you moan,

About anything and everything
And always proved unfit!
So give us a chance, please,
A chance for us to live.

Kerry-Ann Soames (15)
St Paul's Catholic College

FAITH

I heard her crying,
At the sight of the bright light,
I heard him sighing,
At the disappointment of a baby girl,
She was a beautiful thing,
Her skin as white as a pearl.

What he didn't realise, she's still a human being,
No matter whether it's a girl or a boy,
A new life is still worth seeing.
He decided to hold her,
Fragile as though she were,
He stroked her skin, as soft as fur.

He held her hand, it was cold,
He watched to see if she took her breath,
Little did he realise she'd met her death.
How could it be?
She didn't live long enough to become
Familiar with me.

I was silent all day,
Tears tapped the table,
I didn't know what to say,
All I knew, all I felt was pain.
She was only thirty minutes old,
How could things ever be the same?

I had faith her soul would live on,
God would take care of her
Now that's she's gone.

Sharonjit Mato (17)
The Heathland School

INSIDE MY HEAD

Inside my head there is a
moon and a star glistening
in the dark black sky over a
small silent village.

Inside my head there is a
tornado that has destroyed
over 1,000 homes in a furious
frenzy so that even the houses
can't be repaired.

Inside my head there is a
river with clean water and
birds singing and the sun
shining with a smile and a
royal blue sky.

Inside my head there is a
candle which lays unlit in
a small dark room.

Inside my head there is a
silent haunted house next
to a fairy tale house which
is painted with gingerbread walls.

Inside my head there is a
plain field covered with
normal green grass.

Javaid Mohun (11)
The Heathland School

Inside My Head

Inside my head there is a thunderstorm about to explode,
A volcano erupting.
A sudden light comes dashing into my head,
The dynamite stops,
The volcano dies down,
The light sparkles.

Inside my head there is a rainbow with a pot of gold at the end of it.
My thoughts swim around;
My dreams;
My hopes;
My ambitions.

Inside my head there is a football instead of my brain,
I can only think about football.
A book appears and I start to think about homework,
I can't think of anything else . . .
It's like a hamster trying to get out of a cage.

Inside my head there is a thunderstorm about to arrive,
Yet it's near the end of the school day,
And the sun comes out.

James Bavington (11)
The Heathland School

Winter

The last of the autumn leaves have been buried by the snow,
Autumn has packed his cases and is ready to go.
Autumn waves goodbye,
When winter arrives the ground turns white and so does the sky.

Winter opens his case and as he does everything becomes still,
Out comes snow, mist and a terrifying chill.
The snowflakes falling from above, look like stars from space,
Each one has its own individual face.

The snow makes a soft bed
For all the plants and trees which will be dead.
Winter strips the land of everything green,
He thinks he is making it clean.

Spring comes to the rescue
And turns the sky blue.
Spring says, 'Winter leave, you've got the sack.'
'Very well' winter replies, 'but always remember I'll be back.'

Hafsa Ali (13)
The Heathland School

THE DUSTBIN

The dustbin is a smelly place,
With a yucky, mucky, stinky trace.
The dustbin is full of nasty things,
Including egg shells and left-over chicken wings.
The dustbin is also a useful matter,
With a very large mess to scatter.

The dustbin has a very short life,
Picked each week and dropped in a strife.
Food hanging out everywhere;
Banana peels,
Objects not wanting to be feeled.
Raggy clothes,
Grass that's just been mowed.
Empty boxes,
Stuff that looks like it's been chewed by foxes.

The dustbins aren't nice places to go near,
But when you do, don't approach with fear.
The dustbin can be a useful object,
Use it wisely, don't neglect it.

Shilpa Farma (12)
The Heathland School

ELEPHANT HUNTING

He aimed the gun and fired,
The bullet shot out through the whistling wind.
As it hit the thick skin the elephant
Staggered to the ground, with a big *crash*,
The skies thundered with rage.
The elephant took his last breath as he lay there still;
The fierce hunter approached the rest of the herd,
He aimed the gun again and pulled the trigger, *boom*.
The earth shuddered under the great creature,
The alarming predator approached the elephants with a chainsaw,
As he pulled the string the roaring sound chased away the
                                        remaining elephants;
The earth quivered with fear.
Soon after the African plains were left with nothing but two
                                        rotting bodies.

Navjot Dhatt (11)
The Heathland School

INSIDE MY HEAD

Inside my head there is,
A basketball spinning,
If it stops spinning I will freeze.
A dictionary,
Still not complete as I have not come across
All the words in the English language.

Inside my head there is,
A thunderstorm,
I'm not able to control it - I need to think fast.
A whole new me,
An inventor,
A sportsman,
A teacher.

Inside my head there is,
A sunny day awaiting for me,
Everything standing beside me,
Not in front, behind or away from me.

Inside my head there is,
A book about my future
Kept locked and I look at it.
A clock ticking loudly,
When there is silence.

Saif Alqasim (11)
The Heathland School

LOVE

Love is near,
Love is far,
Love is hard to find,
Love can be tempting
Or even a disaster.
If you find someone to love
Then you should feel all warm inside.
Though that person is yours to love,
If it's right, if it's wrong
You decide.
For I have found love
And love has found me.
I hope we stay
Together for ever and ever
For I love thee.

Harpreet Iota (11)
The Heathland School

VOLCANOES

There is a sort of rumbling like an elephant
rolling in bed,
Then there was a big bang like a nuclear
bomb set off by humans,
Then something like overheated custard
comes out of a hole,
It comes down very fast like the drivers
in car races,
Then it dries up like golden syrup on
a pancake.
Suddenly the elephant stops,
Everything is in a mess like the syrup just
fell from the table,
Who cleans up? Mother Nature of course!

Umesh Chapaneri (11)
The Heathland School

TORNADO

He comes crashing from the clouds,
A dizzy giant,
Devouring houses whole,
The stealer of souls.

He comes crashing from the clouds,
A dizzy giant,
Luring thunder and lightning to battle
With his legs of jelly.

He comes crashing from the clouds,
A dizzy giant,
Throwing entire buildings
In a rage of fury.

Hiren Dhanecha (13) & Adnan Ahmed (12)
The Heathland School

INSIDE MY HEAD

Inside my head is a forest full of trees
With mysterious thoughts and secrets which keep growing
And make me want to explode just like a volcano.

When I am nervous I feel like there is an earthquake shaking
everything,
And everything goes blank at once, I can't even think straight.
When I have a headache I feel like there is a thunderstorm
waiting to hit me.
There is a maze, everything has to go in and find its way out,
That is the real test of my memory.

Sometimes words get lost for days, weeks, months, years or
even forever,
I know that the older I get the bushes will grow and gradually it is
Going to get harder and take longer to get out.

There is an alarm clock that keeps on ticking *louder* and *faster,*
When I am running out of time,
And it goes off at exactly 3.30 on days I have to go to school.

Whenever I get a shock a jack-in-the-box pops up.
When I do a good deed I feel as if there is a white ring on top of
my head.

When I have a good idea a light bulb lights up on the top of my head.
When I am hot I feel all dizzy and I feel like the sun would
swallow me up.

Lena Patel (12)
The Heathland School

In My Head

In my head,
I think of the world wars and peace.
I think of Bosnia, Iraq, Ireland and Punjab.
I think of Indonesia, China, Russia and Pakistan,
I think of America, Australia, England and Germany,
I think of the soldiers, their families and pray for peace,
Worrying thoughts in my head.

In my head,
I think of natural disasters,
I think of tornadoes, hurricanes and lightning,
I think of landslides, avalanches and earthquakes,
I think of devastation, despair and total destruction,
I think of old people, parents' children and babies,
I think of those dead, and those living but lost,
Compassionate and desperate thoughts in my head.

In my head,
It's like a tornado sucking up everything along its way,
I think millions of thoughts, some long, others short,
Some remembered, others forgotten,
Some cherished, others discarded,
Some happy, some sad,
Some tender, others rough,
Some warm, others cold,
Some hilarious, others serious,
Just millions of thoughts in my head.

In my head,
I think of water fights on a hot summer's day,
I think of cricket, roller-blading and cycling,
I think of decorating cakes and biscuits,
I think of shopping for my needs and wants,
I think of mums' cuddles, loving, warm and supportive,
I think of home, bed and safety,
I thank God in my head.

Surekha Dhanjal (11)
The Heathland School

A SUNNY DAY

A sunny day is beautiful,
A sunny day is when the flowers
open up like umbrellas,
A sunny day is when the sun looks
like a golden coin,
A sunny day is when the sky is as clear
as the sea beneath us,
A sunny day is as green as the grass
in the fields we walk on,
A sunny day is like ice-cream
melting in our mouths.

Priya Khendria (13)
The Heathland School

ME

Me,
What makes me me?
What makes me be me?
I've got a brain in me,
But that controls the body of me,
Not me!

Me,
What makes me me?
What makes me be me?
I have things inside of me,
But they just help me live.
Not me!

Me,
What makes me me?
What makes me be me?
Me and my friends like having fun,
But that isn't about me.
Not me!

Me,
What makes me me?
What makes me be me?
I have feelings in me,
That is me.
Me!

Me,
What make me me?
What makes me be me?
I have emotions in me,
That is me.
Me!

Me,
What makes me me,
What makes me being me.
I also have a life in me,
That is definitely me.
Me!

Veerinder Singh Kahllon (13)
The Heathland School

POCKET POEM!

This is what I found in my pocket today . . .

A chewed up old bacon buttie left for
a year. *Yuk!*

A two-year-old lollipop that had been
covered in McDonald's tomato ketchup. Sickening!

An Orbit chewing gum that had been smothered
in fungus. Refreshing!

A blood-soaked tissue from last year.

Prawn cocktail, crisp crumbs left mouldy. Crispy!

A chocolate bar, melting and squashed. Yum!

A flattened peanut butter sandwich from tea yesterday. Yuk!

A picture of Mummy and Daddy when they were toddlers.
Huggy love!

A picture of me when I was a baby. *Ahhh!*

That's how dirty I am!

Laura Relle Lee-Ann Piper (11)
Uxbridge High School

NIGHT DREAMS

It's dark in my room tonight,
As dark as a cave late at night.
I go to my window, what do I see?
A star is winking down at me.
I listen downstairs,
Mum shouts up 'Do you want an apple or pear?'
'Neither,' I said,
As I went back to bed.

I dreamt I could fly,
Up, up, ever so high.
I played with the birds and sat on a cloud,
And the birds were singing ever so loud.

I woke up next morn,
I said 'Have the puppies been born?'
'No,' Mum said,
'Go back to bed.'
I looked out the kitchen window,
And there on the sill of the window
Sat a dove,
Those I do love.
I thought 'That is who I shall play with tonight,
When I'm sleeping in bed late tonight.'

Zoe Evans (11)
Uxbridge High School

POST BOX

I am a post box,
I am a very lucky box,
People feed me
Until I am quite full,
But there's one problem,
The postman!
He opens my tummy
Every Thursday
And pulls out my insides
He puts them in a little bag,
And drives off in his car.
For a while I'm hungry,
But I have friends
That come and feed me
So I am happy,
Except every Thursday
When *he* comes!

I am a post box,
A not so very lucky box,
I have been moved
To a village,
A very small village,
With a very small population,
Now I get hungry,
Now not many people feed me,
Now I am sad
There is one good thing
Now I have few letters,
Now *he* doesn't come!

James Sizeland (11)
Uxbridge High School

MY LIFE

I'm sick and tired. You are all so selfish.
I always let you grow fruit on me,
I always let you come under me when it rains,
I always let you come under me when it's too hot.
I let you lie against me when you're tired,
And I give you oxygen!
But what do *you* all do?
You split me up from my friends,
You pull off my emerald green leaves,
And you crack all my
Branches.
You swing
On my branches,
And it's
Not funny!
It does hurt!
But worst of
All, you chop my
Friends down and
Kill us! It's just not
Fair!

Satvir Sihota (11)
Uxbridge High School

THE SEA

The sea is a place of calm
A breeze running through a palm,
I think it's the best place to be,
I can see it in my mind, the *sea!*
Gentle as a baby,
Or it may be.
A strange creature under the sea,
It can be dangerous for you and me.

A thing that eats you, a monster,
Or something pinching you, a lobster
The sea is a place of calm
A breeze running through a palm.

Mojahid Ali (11)
Uxbridge High School

JEALOUSY

I get this feeling inside me
like a blazing fire out of control,
It boils over like a rushing stream.
I get this feeling if I see her,
If she's got something new,
I get very angry,
which is something I don't normally do.
Real life slips into fantasy,
and I dream that the girl riding the new bike is me.
When I first got this feeling, I didn't really care,
but now the feeling is very strongly there.
I can't control this feeling,
it just boils up inside,
I get taken
on a magic roller-coaster ride.
I go over streams of fire,
and streams of silk,
but wherever I go,
the feeling's always there.
I'm jealous because she's rich,
I didn't use to care,
but now,
the feeling's very strongly there.

Nadine Dawes (11)
Uxbridge High School

WHAT AM I?

I lurk in the deep
Waiting and waiting.

I wait for my prey
to come gliding past,
so I can attack.

I pass through corals
below a shoal of fish

I secretly wait for the
time to come
I'm the killer of the deep

You guessed it,
I'm a *s h a r k!*

Charlene Jane Kennedy (11)
Uxbridge High School

DRAGONS!

A dragon is a flying machine,
An ugly looking thing
A wild dinosaur.
A dragon can munch a house
Or blow down a school,
It kills anything in its way.

When a dragon opens its mouth
It causes a storm,
Its fiery tail is alight,
Its teeth are razor-sharp
Its claws will make a path.

Luke Nash (11)
Uxbridge High School

GRANDAD

The world is turning without me
Left me, forgotten me, gone on without me
I sit here alone, in my rotted chair
With only memories to comfort me
No one to talk to, no one to listen
No one to care about the way I live my life.

I sit here watching the world go by,
Watching people go past my window,
Not knowing that beyond that window
Is a man on his own with his memories
Memories about the days of soldiers
When I fought in the Second World War
Memories about me and my wife
And long days out with the children
Now I sit here all alone
Where no one knows about my life
Or the way I feel about my past
And my life flashing before my eyes
So I just sit here, all alone
Watching the world go by
Even though I'm not there,
The world will keep turning.
The Earth will keep spinning and
                              life will go on
And I'll just sit here, watching it go by,
Sitting in my old rotted chair.

Jennifer Smith (13)
Uxbridge High School

REJECTION

I used to be a human,
But now I am on my own.
In my world, there is just one.
Me, just me!

What I need to know is, what really lives inside of me?
It's the question I need an answer to.
Is it the feeling of loneliness wrapped in a ring of warmth
Eating my cold and rejected body?

How does it feel to be loved?
I don't know.
Maybe cold, and deserted in a blue world
As no one, and nothing comes across this blue world,
But for one. One rejected one.

Whatever the feeling I behold, I will always know that
I used to be a human,
But now I am on my own.
In my world, there is just one.
Me, just rejected me.

Natasha Holmes (13)
Uxbridge High School

SEA

The sea laps gently upon the shore
Dragging down pebbles - it's everyday chore
With tiny white hands it takes away stones,
Pieces of litter, driftwood and bones.

So much water, but yet, undrinkable.
In some parts of the world, you are unsinkable!
A watery desert, an untamed place,
A desolate landscape, much like space.

Mark Harris (11)
Uxbridge High School

HIDDEN FEAR

The other day, I was going to sleep,
I was as scared as could be,
I looked outside the window
And a tree was staring at me!

I got more frightened,
So I hid under the bed.
I saw one of my toys talking
I tried to get out and banged my head.

I hid inside my quilt.
I held my teddy bear
Then I felt something
Pulling on my hair.

Aaarrrrgggghhhh! I shouted
While running out the door,
Jumped downstairs
And onto the floor.

I didn't go back
Until the next day
Looked around and
        slept away.

Shamadul Haque (11)
Uxbridge High School

I'M YOUR BED

I'm there for you when you fall asleep,
I'm there for you when you cry and weep.
Sometimes you smell so sweet
Sometimes I wonder about the smell of your feet.
I never move, I'm always there
For some people I'm king size
For some people, I'm square.
You dress me in coloured sheets
You dress me nice and neat.
Sometimes you're heavy and tired
And sometimes you're admired.
You leave me in such a mess
Suppose it's when you're in a hurry, I guess.

Hardeesh Phull (11)
Uxbridge High School

IMAGINATION

As I sit all alone in a pitch-black room,
I hear noises which make me feel like I'm
sitting in a tomb.
I feel terrified to move and to even breathe
I sit so awfully still that you would think I'm dead.
Tiny droplets of sweat trickle down my frozen face,
while my eyes are alert to any frightening face.
I imagine devils and dead souls gathering around me.
I feel their presence pulling me towards a fiery burning door.
I scream and shout and struggle to get out of their
deadly mouldy arms, but it's too late.
I have become one of them.

Ruby Chand (13)
Uxbridge High School

LOVE IS . . .

Love is patient,
Love is kind,
Love is never wrong,
Love is always right,
Love is strong, as strong as steel,
Love is an emotion, the way people feel.

Love is shy,
But love conquers all,
Love survives anything,
Love will never fall.
Love requires nothing but a person to receive it,
Love may seem a small thing but everybody needs it.

Love is oblivious
To what's going on around,
Love ignores everything,
Every noise, every sound.
Every bang, shudder, every sudden twist,
As far as love's concerned, hate will never exist.

Love is a wonder,
A wonder we all adore,
Love is something special,
Need I say anymore?
In short, quite frankly, without love we'd be lost,
Love is one thing on this Earth that can't be
                                bought at any cost.

Lauren Sirey (13)
Uxbridge High School

LIGHT AND DARK

Light

The illumination of my bright morning star!
Shining, gleaming with its radiant shine at the crack of dawn.
The great lush firelight, I look and glare
Strike a light, flame, should I say?
The lambency I feel all day.

The lamplight is gleaming
The moon is glowing
Daylight hours begin
The horrific gaslight I see
Which sparks lights in authority.

Dark:

Now the *night* begins

Nights of light so soon become
Wild and free
I could feel the sun

The dim disturbing air
Fills the place within
With joyless places where
Tension begins.

Nupinder Bhogal (11)
Uxbridge High School

A Whole New World

A whole new world where nobody
feels lonely,
A whole new world where everybody
is friends and no one fights,
A whole new world where everyone
has enough food.
A whole new world where everyone
has equal rights.
A whole new world that everybody
is part of.
A whole new world where nobody
lives on the streets.
A whole new world is where
we should live!

Lauren Noble (11)
Uxbridge High School

The Waterful Fountain

The tint of blue in the
waterful
fountain
Makes it look like a mountain
The colours are passionate
Like a deep blue sky
It's a fountainful sight to see
The splashes of light
And we come to the
waterful
fountain

Annie Smith (11)
Uxbridge High School